MIND DETOX

MIND DETOX

DISCOVER AND RESOLVE THE ROOT CAUSES
OF CHRONIC CONDITIONS
AND PERSISTENT PROBLEMS

SANDY C. NEWBIGGING

 FINDHORN PRESS

Findhorn Press
One Park Street
Rochester, Vermont 05767
www.findhornpress.com

SUSTAINABLE FORESTRY INITIATIVE   Certified Sourcing
www.sfiprogram.org
SFI-00854

Text stock is SFI certified

Findhorn Press is a division of Inner Traditions International

Disclaimer

The information in this book is given in good faith and is neither intended to diagnose any physical or mental condition nor to serve as a substitute for informed medical advice or care. The author of this book does not dispense medical advice nor prescribe the use of any food or technique as a form of treatment for medical problems. Please contact your health professional for medical advice and treatment. Neither author nor publisher can be held liable by any person for any loss or damage whatsoever which may arise directly or indirectly from the use of this book or any of the information therein.

Cataloging-in-Publication Data for this title is available from the Library of Congress

ISBN 978-1-62055-833-1 (print)
ISBN 978-1-62055-834-8 (ebook)

Printed and bound in the United States by Lake Book Manufacturing, Inc. The text stock is SFI certified. The Sustainable Forestry Initiative® program promotes sustainable forest management.

10 9 8 7 6 5 4 3 2 1

Edited by Jacqui Lewis
Text design and layout by Damian Keenan
Illustration by Richard Crookes
This book was typeset in Adobe Caslon Pro and Calluna Sans with Calluna Serif used as a display typeface.

To send correspondence to the author of this book, mail a first-class letter to the author c/o Inner Traditions • Bear & Company, One Park Street, Rochester, VT 05767, and we will forward the communication, or contact the author directly at **www.sandynewbigging.com**

Contents

. . .

CASE-STUDY "success stories" have been gathered from the author's consultation notes between 2005 and 2012 and from the case notes of independent Mind Detox Method (MDM) practitioners. Client names have been changed to respect privacy. All case studies from independent MDM practitioners have been used with gratitude and on faith that they accurately reported the outcomes. Wordings of comments have been edited slightly for readability purposes only.

Third Time Lucky?

· · · · · ·

THE SECOND EDITION

I CANNOT WRITE. *I am going to let people down.* I first wrote about Mind Detox in my fifth book, *Peace for Life*, which I self-published in 2011. Despite having already worked with publishers, I opted to self-publish at the time to maintain editorial control because I felt my voice had been edited out of my previous two books. But not long after *Peace for Life* was released, Findhorn Press asked me to write three books with them and I felt encouraged, as they were keen to keep them as close to my original manuscripts as possible.

Having heard about the power of Mind Detox and with a genuine desire to help it to get out to a larger audience, they asked that one of the trilogy was about the method. So we wrote and published *Heal the Hidden Cause* in 2013. I thought that was the end of the story, but in the spirit of much of what's shared within this book: life doesn't always happen how we think it will.

In late 2017, I was contacted again by Findhorn Press to tell me that they had merged with another publisher, and would I like to take it as an opportunity to write a second edition. I said yes, but in that moment also had the immediate intuitive *hit* that it was time to call it *Mind Detox*. They agreed and here it is, for you, but not without a few unexpected challenges along the way.

As it is my twelfth published book, I wanted *Mind Detox* to be like none other I've written. Soon after agreeing to write about the method for a third time, I had the scary realization that, to do the method justice and to offer something new, it was time to include personal stories that I'd never been brave enough to tell before.

You see, I've been there and got the torn t-shirt to prove it. I'm not preaching from the sidelines as I've detoxed my own mind, a lot. I've been super-low, super-anxious, super-sick, and felt super-stuck and unsuccessful. I've been in dark places during my life and got dirty in the pit, but I've also been lucky enough to have ways to get out of the other side; more cleansed, healed and happier than ever.

I'm also much more aware these days about the power of storytelling. Stories relax us, soothe us and open our hearts and minds to new possibilities and experiences. Stories are, as a result, an incredible tool for making positive changes to our inner and outer worlds. By watching, listening to or reading stories, deep parts of us, which we may not be aware of ever existing, are accessed and can be changed for the better. I hope that, by sharing stories about my "private" life and Mind Detox work, it helps you with yours.

Has it been easy to be so honest? No. As I sat down to write this book I discovered something about myself that I had been living unaware of for many years. Quite innocently, I'd been presenting only my best image to the world. I'd been representing myself as a guy who's always had *all* of his shit together. And to a large extent, I really *do* live with a great amount of peace, joy and laughter and I have enjoyed success in what I do.

However, there have also been some parts of me that I've withheld and kept a secret. Parts that I did not love, and so I would, without realizing, fail to show them to anyone, in fear that they didn't love these parts of me too.

This undercover reluctance to share *all* parts of myself meant I experienced writer's block for the first time in my entire book-writing career. Then, after a few months of artfully avoiding sitting down to write, I ended up down to the last four weeks before the most recent, absolutely final, deadline. Sitting at my laptop, I decided to open up Facebook to delay the inevitable a little longer. At the top of my newsfeed was a lovely picture of a mentoring client of mine; all smiles, holding her baby.

Why is this relevant, and how did seeing the picture help me to overcome the writer's block and get the book done on time? The client originally wanted to work with me because she was single, childless, turning 40 and believed she would never meet anyone, let alone have a family. So we did Mind Detox over a few mentoring sessions to discover and resolve the possible causes of her relationship difficulties. When I saw her picture on Facebook, I hadn't heard from her in over a year since our last meeting.

Looking at her beaming face, with her newborn child in her arms and loving partner nearby, reawakened something inside me. I remembered why I do this work – to improve lives and help the world to be a happier, kinder and more peaceful place. It reminded me to not play small; to make my purpose more important than any false fears. It also reminded me that she is one of thousands of lives that have become better by using Mind Detox. It motivated me to take a big deep breath, be ruthlessly real and do whatever it takes to get this method into as many hands and hearts as possible, so that anyone can learn how to turn their difficulties into the life of their dreams.

Sandy C. Newbigging,
January 2019

The Incurable Cured

· · · · · ·

BY SASHA ALLENBY, BEST-SELLING
AUTHOR OF *MATRIX REIMPRINTING USING EFT*

I CANNOT HEAL. *Whatever I do to get better doesn't work.*
When I started out on my journey of transforming two incurable long-term health conditions, I had no concept of the role that healing my underlying emotional issues would play in my return to health. Despite an open mind and an interest in holistic therapies, at the time of my sickness, I was still locked in the current popular western medical paradigm that something had gone "wrong" with my body, that it had "failed" me in some way and that I needed some kind of outside intervention to "fix" it. I didn't make even a tenuous link between the myriad life stresses, left unresolved and pushed down while I wore a mask of happiness on the surface, and the breakdown in my physiology. Despite trying a whole host of physical interventions spanning several years, it wasn't until I addressed the underlying emotional causative factors of my disease that my body healed, and when it did, the change was dramatic.

From Bed-Bound to Brilliant Health

The fact that I went from complete bed-bound disability to total health in a relatively short space of time may seem miraculous, but what I have witnessed and supported in others since actually makes it seem quite commonplace to me now. Inspired by my own transformation, and passionately wanting to share what I had learned, I went on to build an international client base, supporting thousands worldwide through my own practice and training courses. I also co-authored a book with the creator of a technique built on the very foundations that *Mind Detox* rests upon: resolve the underlying emotional factors to a physical condition, and the body heals accordingly.

Time and again I saw people from all walks of life turn around a whole host of physiological and psychological issues, or at least gain a vast improvement in their symptoms, when they addressed the specific underlying emotional factors to physical diseases, alongside the accompanying beliefs that were holding their body in a diseased state. I saw people transform everything from cancer to diabetes, bipolar affective disorder to chronic fatigue syndrome, rheumatoid arthritis to post-traumatic stress disorder, eczema to phobias, to name but a few, until eventually the miraculous became normalized.

Simple Solution for Remarkable Results

Throughout this journey I have always been interested in creating, developing and researching tools and techniques that enable quick and lasting shifts in the emotional climate, and which enable the body and mind to return to a healthful state. So it was with great interest that I was introduced to Sandy C. Newbigging's Mind Detox method. For me, one of the key factors underlying the success of this method is its simplicity. This makes it highly accessible to both practitioners who want to help their clients quickly uncover the root cause of a condition and to lay people who want to get to the heart of their own challenges. But don't be fooled by the simplicity of this method. The results of this technique are remarkable, and can be seen time and again in Sandy's thousands of clinical hours with clients.

Mind Detox is more than just another technique to trans-form the emotions; Sandy has built a whole system based on working with real people and the challenges that they face. So *Mind Detox* does more than deliver a technique for transformation and self-help. What I have experienced in my own practice and with the countless practitioners I have trained is that it is one thing to present a technique, but another thing altogether to address the deep underlying blocks that people face when they are using this technique to create changes for themselves. *Mind Detox* does just that, not only presenting an accessible system that can be used by all but also highlighting a whole host of solutions to the blocks that people encounter when they are making personal changes.

There are some real gems in this book, from the in-depth exploration of how to identify and resolve the underlying core beliefs that are contributing to sickness and disease, to the new ways of perceiving the past, which highlights common blocking beliefs to creating transformation and how to move through them.

A Genuinely Helpful Self-Help Book

Mind Detox is a book that is beneficial to all. It is for practitioners who want to support a deeper healing journey with their clients. Its accessibility also makes it the book that practitioners can give to their clients so they can better understand their own healing journey. It can also be given to a friend or a relative to demonstrate how they can impact their own healing. Perhaps most importantly, it is the book that you can use on yourself time and time again, as you deepen your understanding of how your mind and body are linked and put the tools in this book into practice on yourself. If you not only read this book but also consistently apply Mind Detox to yourself, it can enable you to join the many ranks of people who have experienced the miraculous in their healing journey by addressing their unresolved emotional challenges. I wish you peace as your journey with Mind Detox unfolds.

The Peace Prize

· · · · · ·

MIRACLE OR METHOD?

WHERE IS MY BABY? *Is there something wrong?* My tired mum anxiously asked. "You said you'd bring him back for feeding hours ago, but nobody's brought him, I'm worried that he must be hungry by now." This is the conversation that my mum had with a nurse, hours after giving birth to me. The run-up to that moment was also a super-stressful time, for both of my parents. I tried to come early and my mum had labour pains for several weeks. When I did finally arrive I was a very big baby, ten pounds to be precise. Chubby would be an understatement, and as I was a rather worrying colour of blue, the hospital staff promptly removed me from my mother's arms to get extra oxygen, and then on to the nursery.

This was my welcome to the world. Being taken from my mum to spend hours alone without care and food. It didn't matter that it was an innocent oversight by the hospital staff. I didn't know that then. My upset feelings came from my perhaps natural, yet misinformed perceptions, which were fuelled by what I *thought* had happened. Without knowing the reality of the situation, I continued my life unaware of the event ever happening, along with the toxic belief that had been unconsciously created that day. Subsequently, I had no idea the event and belief had been screwing with my life, from behind the scenes, for several years. It wasn't until I did a Mind Detox (over three decades later) that the ramifications of being left alone after my birth were finally revealed and resolved.

Life On My Island of Loneliness

I lived with an underlying angst that I was alone in the world and ultimately unwanted. It didn't matter how often people said they loved me or that they wanted me around, I never believed it, and acted accordingly. Inwardly I existed like an island, feeling lonely, left out, isolated and unworthy of love. I created a range of corrosive coping strategies that ended up ruining the majority of my relationships. I believed that I was bothering people with my mere presence. The ways I felt and acted also messed with my ability to make money and limited other areas of my life, too.

Using the simple yet profound method outlined within this book, I discovered that my birth made me feel "*Sad, scared and alone because I'm not wanted*". It made sense, seeing as that was how I'd secretly felt for most of my life. Despite it being obvious, up to this point I had been completely oblivious to carrying this emotionally charged incorrect conclusion around with me, until the day I did Mind Detox. Through the process I was able to get peace with the past event by acknowledging that my parents *did* actually want me; in fact they never wanted me to be taken away from them in the first place. There was no reason to be scared because I was reunited, fed, taken care of and ultimately, I survived. Taking on board these "knowings" from my older and wiser present-day self, I felt calm when recalling the past series of events surrounding my birth and my underlying chronic loneliness dissolved. This also caused the old toxic belief of being unwanted to have no legs to stand on and to lose its power to adversely impact me any longer.

I've since learned that even if we begin life with no spoken words, we are able to feel what's going on from before our first breath. Later in life, we learn to use words to convey how we feel – but feelings are fuelling the formation of our beliefs from the get-go. As most of our strong beliefs are created before our teenage years, during a period in our life when we have little life experience, they are often misinformed and downright wrong. Meaning that even the earliest of events can impact our entire life – unless we proactively discover our misinformed beliefs and update them. This is what the Mind Detox method is essentially for, and why it has positively impacted thousands of lives worldwide.

We have all had challenging events happen to us, and as a consequence, formed a few incorrect conclusions that are working against us being the healthiest, happiest and most successful versions of our self. With this book you can heal the hidden parts of your mind that have been secretly hindering you, and move forward with more freedom and fulfilment.

> *Mind Detox gives us the ability to live our best life today; without unresolved stuff from the past pulling us back.*

Giving Birth to My Own Method

Fresh out of university with a big desire brewing in my belly to make a positive difference, I had a chance encounter with a life coach and decided to train as one myself. Despite graduating at the top of my class, I noticed that even when my clients agreed upon strong success strategies, they would often return with their tail between their legs saying that they couldn't actually bring themselves to *do* what we had agreed. It became clear that their unresolved past "stuff", i.e. negative emotions, limiting beliefs and habitual behaviour patterns were preventing them, big time.

Motivated to find ways of working deeper, I sought out more systems of self-transformation to add to my coaching toolkit, including the Emotional Freedom Technique (EFT) and Neuro Linguistic Programming (NLP). After a few years of successfully offering coaching with a therapeutic twist, I received an invitation that led to a series of surprising events, which resulted in me giving birth to my own method.

I was invited to work as a therapist on a detox health retreat in southern Spain. With no idea of what to expect (at that time I thought detox was only for drug addicts!), I packed my bag and headed off for a week in the sun. It rained heavily the entire time! I'm not sure if it was the weather that week or what, but my therapy schedule quickly became fully booked.

In more ways than just the location, I found myself in unfamiliar territory. Many of the detoxers were attending the retreat because they were suffering from chronic conditions. During that week I was to meet people suffering with migraines, irritable bowel syndrome (IBS), infertility, bulimia, obesity and psoriasis. This meant that not only was I suddenly working in the field of "health", but also, due to my busy schedule, I only had a limited amount of time with each of them.

A Fortunate Coincidence

Two weeks prior to going to Spain I had been invited to a talk by Dr David R. Hamilton, an ex-scientist and expert in the mind–body connection. (Come to think of it, on another very wet day, this time just outside Glasgow, Scotland.) During that mind-blowing talk, David shared a whole host of scientific studies that had investigated the power of the mind–body connection, including the mind's ability to heal the body.

With his message springing to the forefront of my own mind a couple of weeks later in Spain, I knew I had to update my approach, fast. Clutching at straws, but wanting to do what I could to help, I knew that I *was* able to assist the detoxers with their mental and emotional health. With no clue as to where the coaching session might go, I suggested to my first client that we explore whether there might be any unresolved issues from their past that could be causing their physical problems today. With their agreement we proceeded.

Hmmm, To My Next Question...

I had no idea what to ask! I remember looking down at my blank notebook and then up again to meet the expectant eyes of my client. I decided to keep it simple by asking if there was an event in her life that might be causing her health condition, such that if we were to resolve it, the body would heal.

To both of our amazements, she instantly had an answer; a memory had "popped into her mind". With the help of a few more questions, we could see a possible link between the unresolved past event and her current condition. Once we had established the possible mind-based cause, we then spent the rest of our time together getting peace with the past memory and the session was done.

Time after time, in session after session, this happened with great success. Over the coming months I regularly witnessed remissions from health conditions; I saw skin conditions clear up, chronic pain vanish and digestion problems disappear, to name but a few. I also witnessed the resolution and subsequent improvement of many other emotional issues and life problems, all from doing one thing – making peace with the past.

Lucky Break

News about my method, which by this point was becoming known as "Mind Detox" then spread internationally when I was shown on three separate television series documenting people going through a week-long mind–body detox retreat. During these televised retreats, many thousands of viewers were able to watch people from all backgrounds cure a range of common health conditions – by taking a holistic approach to healing. The media exposure and subsequent book deals led to the opportunity of working with countless Mind Detox clients at my clinics, workshops and retreats internationally.

It's a Miracle! (Or Is It?)

Over time I became curious. Was I witnessing to miracles? Was I some kind of gifted healer? Or had I simply stumbled across a method of healing chronic conditions and persistent life problems that could be transferable and used by others?

Over the following year I started using the same series of questions to discover and resolve the mind-based cause(s) of my clients' various issues. Quickly it became evident that the power of the method was the method itself. This was exciting especially as I couldn't be everywhere people needed the method and there's only a limited number of hours a day in which I could personally do Mind Detox sessions. For more people to benefit, the method being used without my direct involvement was an absolute must. This also presented the opportunity of creating a network of trained practitioners; so I founded an academy and started training and certifying others in the Mind Detox method.

Somebody somewhere is benefiting from Mind Detox today.

Transcending the Torment of Mental Toxicity

Mind Detox is a proven way to find and fix the possible mind-based causes of physical, emotional and life problems. If something negative is happening in your body or your life and you don't know why, then this method can help. It enables you to get peace with the past and, in doing so, update any misinformed beliefs that have been messing with your physical wellness, mental positivity and life success. You will learn that when you change your mind, by perceiving your past, present and future in a more positive light, the body can heal and life improve, quickly.

As the name suggests, Mind Detox is a tool for *letting go* of anything toxic that is preventing you from being at your best. I believe we are born with brilliance built in, but if we are holding on to unresolved stuff from the past, it is harder to engage our natural states of inner peace and immense potential. Whether it is hurt, rejection, anger, resentment, guilt, grief, fear or sadness, for example, you can let go and be clear of it all, to the point that your past no longer limits you, or causes you upset, stress or suffering.

> *Mind Detox is a way to finally forgive and find peace, which is required for reclaiming our power, peace and potential.*

Freed from the torment of mental toxicity, we are clear-headed, open hearted, heroic humans. With no excess baggage to carry, we do what we came here to do, and with a zest and love for life. We are a peaceful, proactive and positive presence in the world.

Mind Detox is also pleasantly direct, going quickly to the root of any issue, and doesn't involve years of therapy. It is the go-to tool for people needing to get peace with the past and who know that their mind is standing in the way of their success.

Pure Perception and The Peace Prize

Peace with the past is possible. I know this from successfully Mind Detoxing hundreds of people, many of whom had rather extreme events and experiences needing resolved. How we perceive past events determines whether we endure problems or experience peace. Are we looking through a mental lens that is clouded by toxic assumptions, beliefs or attitudes? If so, we lack pure perception.

These three elements distort our remembering of things that have happened in our past and justify a reactive resistance towards what we *think* happened. The combination of impure perception and reactive resistance creates chronic stress, negative emotions, problematic behavioural patterns and, in some cases, ill-health. In short, if there is an absence of peace with the past, then we can be sure there is also an absence of pure perception.

> *Our perceptions are pure when we see the entirety of reality, as it actually is, rather than seeing a falsified edited version of reality, based upon our assumptions, beliefs and attitudes.*

Being at peace with the past requires us to return to the truth of reality, where resolution is waiting for us. Until we do this, our life is defined and determined by a series of fictitious fantasies, imagined by our mind, which are only a relative reality (similar to a dream or convincing story). It is the stories that we make up and tell ourselves *about* life – distorted by our impure perceptions – that hurt and hinder us over time. When we uncover the truth of reality, we automatically and immediately find the hidden treasures of forgiveness, wisdom, understanding and acceptance.

> *"Our eventual fate will be the sum of the stories we told ourselves long enough."*
> — CRYSTAL WOODS

If truth and the prize of peace is what we want, we must be willing to question our assumptions and challenge our beliefs stemming from what we *think* happened. We need to instead see what *really* went on. Mind Detox involves the answering of a series of questions that help us to discover the truth of any given situation and, in doing so, find resolution in the recognition of reality. Before we get into the actual 5-Step Method (in Part Two), here are three introductory questions to ask now to get started:

- Are my facts about what happened actually fictions?
- Is the *real* problem my perceptions of the past?
- Do I want to be right or do I want to be at peace?

Consider a problematic past event within the context of these three initial questions and notice what happens within you. The simple act of questioning your assumptions can crack open an inner door through which peace becomes possible. Little can be done to improve things if you are adamant that the past happened how you currently believe it did. However, if you are open to perceiving your past with fresh eyes and from a more positive and empowered perspective, then Mind Detox can work wonders.

Become Curious About the Cause

In my observations, the causes of many physical, emotional and life circumstantial problems exist within the more subtle (unconscious) realms of the mind. This can make them very difficult to find and fix – unless you know how. With Mind Detox you have a powerful method for doing exactly this, so that you can be free from persistent problems and enjoy a more positive and prosperous life.

With Mind Detox you can find what I call the Root-Cause Reason, which, as you will learn, is justifying the existence of one or more toxic beliefs. I say toxic because, left unresolved; they are a breeding ground for a host of health conditions and life problems. Toxic beliefs are bad for us because they justify inner resistance, which you will learn is a secret source of stress and one of the main reasons why your chronic problem hasn't healed before now.

> *As long as you are resisting, your problem will be persisting.*

Having discovered the Root-Cause Reason (more about that in Chapter 3), the method then helps you to come to healthier conclusions about what happened, which in turn promotes a higher presence of inner harmony *with* whatever you may have been perpetually resisting. Due to the interconnection between your mind, body and external world, reducing resistance and increasing inner peace allows for positive changes to occur within your health and your life circumstances.

Having tracked the harmful conclusions, I have discovered and worked with the most common toxic beliefs. I will reveal what these beliefs are so that you can make sure you don't have any of them – or so that, if you do, you can detox them from your mind. But before we get on to that, here are the primary motivations for people wanting to experience Mind Detox:

1. **CHRONIC CONDITIONS:** *To stop solely treating physical symptoms and instead discover and resolve the possible mind-based Root-Cause Reason(s) for health condition(s)*

2. **EMOTIONAL UNEASE:** *To stop feeling certain negative emotions, such as anger or anxiety, and feel better more often.*

3. **PERSISTENT PROBLEMS:** *To understand why something bad keeps happening, and again, to discover and resolve the possible root causes, so they move on free from problematic life patterns.*

1. Resolve the Root Cause of Chronic Conditions

The physical body frequently speaks the mind in highly symbolic ways, often mirroring our beliefs, attitudes and relationship with life; so as we improve all three with Mind Detox, the body often reflects these improvements. I will share examples of this and success stories in Chapters 1–4, but suffice to say, the goal with this method is to have such a pure, buoyant and balanced inner climate that any chronic health conditions simply cannot continue.

Stress is also widely regarded as being the most common cause of physical problems on the planet. Perhaps surprisingly though, external people or situations do not cause stress. Instead, our inner resistance *to* life does. (I talk more about this in Chapter 3.) Mind Detox finds the hidden justifications that are causing a chronic resistance to certain life events and helps us to live more in harmony *with* our past, present and possible future. As resistance reduces, so does harmful stress, allowing the body to heal more easily. Experiencing more peace, we can discover that harmony heals.

2. Resolve the Root Cause of Emotional Unease

You feel whatever you feel because you *believe it is justified* to feel it. Read that again.

Emotions are driven by the beliefs held within your unconscious mind, meaning they happen without the need for any conscious thought. This is why even though you may want to stop feeling certain emotions, such as anxiety or anger, you can continue to feel them. Your conscious mind, which is the part of your mind that you are aware of, may prefer to feel positive, but as long as the unconscious mind believes it is justified to feel something negative, then that is how you will end up feeling.

With Mind Detox we resolve the unconscious causes of feeling bad so that we naturally feel good, more often.

We achieve this by again recognizing that it is not life events, but our resistance *to* certain life events, that ultimately determines whether we feel good or bad in any given moment. By this rationale, if we want to feel good more often, we need to reactively resist life less. Mind Detox helps us to find and remove the unhelpful assumptions and toxic beliefs that have been secretly *justifying* our chronic resistance to certain life situations. As our inner harmony *with* life rises, feelings of happiness, confidence, peace and love also rise, along with other "positive" emotional states.

3. Resolve the Root Cause of Persistent Life Problems

In a very innocent way, your mind wants to prove your beliefs right. If you have any toxic beliefs relating to your ability to create the life you want, then your mind will do everything it can to make your beliefs a living reality. For example, if you believe that it is hard to make money then your mind will help you to prove that it's hard to make money! Mind Detox uncovers the secret sources of your unhelpful beliefs and then forms positive and productive beliefs about yourself, other people and the world. With a new and improved belief system, your mind then goes to work again, but this time proving your new beliefs right, and life success can become easier.

Mind Detox simplifies therapy, makes self-help helpful and speeds up self-healing – so everyone is able to enjoy the best life.

It's Never Too Late

Our levels of happiness, health, wealth and success are a perfect reflection of our relationship *with* life. If you have an unhealthy relationship with life then you will often resist what happens and feel bad, get stressed and suffer. However, with a healthy relationship with life you live with enhanced inner peace and harmony. In turn, your body endures less harmful stress, your emotions are more naturally upbeat and you are empowered – no longer engaging or enduring a self-limiting mindset. By making peace with your past, your body can heal, and by cleansing toxic beliefs about yourself, others and life, you more easily create the life you want. It's a genuine win-win.

As you use and eventually embody this method, to the point that it becomes automatic, you gain a self-perpetuating peace with anything in the past, present and future. Hindsight speeds up and you get to see the perfection of your life path, as it unfolds. It is so liberating! They say it's never too late to have a happy childhood. I would agree, while also inviting us to not limit it to the past. It's never too late to enjoy a happy life, starting now.

"Healing is a matter of time,
but it is also a matter of opportunity."

HIPPOCRATES

PART ONE

The Mindset

• • • • • •

GET READY FOR REMARKABLE RESULTS

CHAPTER ONE

The Hidden Cause

. . . . . .

HOW TO STOP TREATING SYMPTOMS

I CANNOT EAT. *My throat feels tight and my empty belly feels full.* Whenever I was secretly struggling with a problem, I would lose my appetite. It didn't matter if the plate in front of me was full of my favourite food (pizza, if you're wondering). I would take a bite and feel like I was going to choke with every attempt to swallow. As if a football was filling my stomach, eating was near impossible. My weight would inevitably drop, dramatically, ending up with me being way too skinny, to the point of looking gaunt. I knew my body needed nutrition and would do my very best to eat, but I couldn't bring myself to partake in the simple act of eating. To get to the bottom of it, I explored the unconscious cause with Mind Detox.

"What event in my life is the cause of my eating problem, the first event that, when resolved, will cause the problem to disappear?" I remembered that when I was a baby I was allergic to my mum's milk. I would throw up within minutes of being fed. Concerned for my welfare, my mum took me to the doctor, who told her to keep feeding me her milk as I would still be getting *some* nutrition. This meant, as far as I was concerned, I was essentially being poisoned for the first few months of my life.

What does this have to do with me being unable to eat as an adult, especially when feeling troubled? Using Step 3 of the method it became clear that as a newborn baby I couldn't tell my mum I had a problem. I literally couldn't speak yet! One way I *could* communicate that I had a problem with what I was being fed (apart from crying, of course) was to stop eating. My unconscious mind (which, along with emotions, is also in charge of the majority of our habits and behaviours) learned that not eating was a successful strategy for letting people know that I had a problem. Fast-forward a few years and any time I was secretly struggling with something, I was unable to eat. Until eventually, upon noticing I had lost weight or wasn't eating, someone would ask: "Are you okay?" At which point I would finally find my voice and appetite.

Looking back, it was clear that I now knew my mum was in no way intentionally wanting to cause me any harm whatsoever. In reality, she was very concerned about my welfare and simply doing what her doctor instructed her to do. Now that I *have* learned to speak, I am also able to tell people if something is up with me. Finally, I know that people care about me and are happy to listen if I'm struggling. Since resolving this past memory, my eating disorder has gone and I'm able to speak up much faster and fix things sooner.

· · ·

Stop Treating Surface-Level Symptoms

Conventional approaches to healing chronic conditions and persistent life problems can fail to deliver long-term benefits because they often only treat the surface-level physical symptoms rather than resolve the deeper underlying mental and emotional causes. Ignoring the underlying causes is a bit like attempting to flatten a turbulent river without removing the jagged rocks sitting below the surface. You can try all you like, but without removing the rocks it is going to make very little difference in the long run.

The mind and body are very much one. As a result, physical problems don't necessarily have purely physical causes. Due to the scientifically proven mind–body connection, unresolved emotional events and mental beliefs can also cause physical problems.

> *What your mind believes, perceives and experiences has the potential to be sent to your entire body and cause physical responses.*

The human body is designed to function well. Its prime objective is to do everything it possibly can to survive. It does not go against this goal of optimum wellness without good reason. If you *do* have a problematic health condition then there is also a reason *why*. Meaning that your body will keep creating the condition until the reason(s) for it is removed. If mind-based past "stuff" is playing a role in the creation of your condition, then resolving the mental and emotional reason(s) *why* your condition has been required by your body can obviously help. With no reason(s) for your condition to continue, the body naturally chooses a healthier way to achieve its inherent goal of self-survival, and self-healing happens. It just makes sense.

Using Mind Detox, I regularly witness physical healings occurring, along with dramatic improvements in how people feel and the life success they enjoy, by focusing less on treating symptoms and instead healing the hidden mind-based root causes.

> *When you change your mind for the better, your body responds accordingly, as the mind and body are in constant communication.*

The Disempowered Dilemma

Consider the alternative. If there are no mind-based reasons for health issues, then the reason(s) usually boil down to things like age, bad luck, "wear and tear", "catching the condition" or because it "runs in the family". Reasons like these disempower and limit our ability to take action towards our own sustained health and self-healing. If we truly believe there are only ever physical causes to physical conditions then we inevitably need to rely solely on things like diets, drugs or operations, which can often come with their own negative side-effects or inconveniences. However, if we are open to the cause stemming from something in our mind, which can be changed, then we can most definitely do something about it.

. . .

[I always encourage integrative medicine, so keep talking to doctors and make the most of modern medicine. When doing so, to remain empowered and adopt a holistic strategy, stay aware that the mind and body are one and when we heal the mind, it can help the body to follow – into a more optimum state of health.]

Your Body *Is* Your Mind

The mind–body connection has been known about for centuries, but it is only in recent years that so many scientific studies have been able to prove how thoughts and emotions affect the body:

IF YOU'RE GRATEFUL... then you almost double the efficiency of certain aspects of your immune system, heal more quickly due to higher oxygenation of the tissues and positively impact the "coherence" of your heart rhythms, which can have a positive knock-on effect with many of the other essential organs too.

IF YOU'RE ANGRY... then, as some researchers at Ohio State University found, you get a surge in cytokines, the immune molecules that trigger inflammation. High levels of cytokines are linked with arthritis, diabetes, heart disease and cancer.

IF YOU'RE JEALOUS... then your body ends up suffering from increased blood pressure, heart rate and adrenalin levels, and weakened immunity.

IF YOU'RE IN LOVE... then you increase the levels of nerve-growth factor, according to research at the University of Pavia in Italy. Enhanced nerve growth helps restore the nervous system and improves memory. Love has also been linked with pain relief, healthier hearts and living longer.

IF YOU'RE STRESSED OUT... then a harmful concoction of stress hormones, including adrenalin and norepinephrine, can end up circulating through your body. Over time, stress hormones like these have been found to compromise the immune system, weaken organs, cause the body to turn off long-term building-and-repair projects, speed up the aging process and make the body more prone to developing chronic illness.

The List Goes On...

Having investigated the multitude of ways the mind shows up within the body, it has become blaringly evident that the body is a physical manifestation of whatever is happening in the mind. Your unconscious mind is linked with your autonomic nervous system, which regulates your heartbeat, blood pressure, digestion and metabolism, along with other "automatic" bodily functions.

Obvious autonomic mind–body connection responses include getting a red face when embarrassed, your mouth watering when you think of certain foods and experiencing butterflies in your stomach when you're feeling nervous or excited. Even sexual arousal requires the mind and body to communicate! Although we generally take these common physical reactions based on the mind–body-connection for granted, it's useful to take a moment to appreciate what's really going on.

Your embarrassed red face requires thousands of chemical reactions to take place within your body along with the diversion of blood flow to your skin. That sensation of nervousness in your stomach is the blood draining from the stomach lining as it heads to the outer regions of the body to help you resist or run from the perceived threat. When it comes to sexual arousal – well, we all know that a range of physical responses happen if certain thoughts occur!

Chemical Messengers of the Mind

Many of these examples of the mind–body connection are known due to evidence of the mind being found to exist in the cells of your body. Neuropeptides (which are also known as "the molecules of emotion") are released into your bloodstream, which in turn affect the functioning of your entire body by communicating with your individual cells.

Now there are very few places within your body that you can cut yourself where you wouldn't bleed. Similarly, there are few places in your body where you don't find neuropeptides. The body is literally riddled with the chemical messengers of your thoughts; so much so that it is scientifically accurate to say the state of your body is quite literally a physical manifestation of your mind.

Stop to consider all the physical reactions that happen as a result of what's happening in your thoughts and emotions, and you can't help but begin to question whether your chronic pain, skin condition or digestive disorder, for example, is the result of a purely physical phenomenon.

Proof of Your Self-Healing Power

I've been lucky enough to witness people from around the world heal a wide variety of physical conditions that more conventional thinking would suggest were impossible to cure. I've also been encouraged to see the amazing results attained by the Mind Detox Practitioners and Calmologists whom I've had the privilege to train via my academy.

Over the past few years, people experiencing the methods shared in this book have reported improvements with many chronic physical and emotional conditions, including acid reflux, acne, addictions, allergies, anger, anxiety, asthma, arthritis, back problems, chronic pain, constipation, depression, diabetes, eating disorders, eczema, fatigue, fear, food intolerances, grief, guilt, headaches, hearing loss, hyperhidrosis, insomnia, irritable bowel syndrome, M.E., migraines, panic attacks, psoriasis, phobias, thyroid problems, weight gain and more.

Although no guarantees can be made about healing, if you are experiencing ill-health I have found it to be very helpful to take a holistic approach that includes Mind Detox.

To increase your confidence in what you are about to learn, please read through the benefits and real-life self-healing success stories scattered through the next few chapters. Not only do they make for inspirational reading, they can also help you to develop the belief that self-healing is not only possible, but inevitable, which is paramount for activating your body's inbuilt self-healing capabilities. On top of that, they can help to illustrate that we can potentially stop treating symptoms by resolving the mind–body connection causes.

BENEFIT NO.1 Pain-Free Without Painkillers

The body speaks the mind. If something causes emotional pain, then it can eventually lead to physical pain. I've seen chronic pain vanish instantly when a person finds peace with their past.

• • •

Meet John, who had back pain:

> "Ever since a car accident over two years ago I had been
> suffering from a painful lower back. After a conversation

with Sandy we discovered the root cause of why my back was vulnerable in the first place, which linked back to when my dad went into hospital for a few weeks when I was a child. When I resolved it, the pain went away immediately. That night I slept through with no painkillers (for the first time in over two years) and got up the next morning and did yoga!"

• • •

Meet Gail, who had painful knees:

"I had been suffering with very painful and swollen knees for many months, so I met up with Sandy to receive a Mind Detox consultation. I was amazed by the results.

The pain eased immediately, and by the following day the swelling had gone down and I was able to wear my beloved three-inch heels again. I am still pain-free and trotting around in my heels. Mind Detox is fantastic."

• • •

Meet Kate, who also had knee problems:

"After a kneecap dislocation, I found myself experiencing extreme pain every time I tried to move my knee, making physiotherapy, and therefore recovery, impossible.

Through working with a pain specialist physiotherapist I came to realize that my knee did not actually physically hurt at all, but that there was a psychological reason for the pain I was feeling. I had a session with Sandy where he quickly identified that the original dislocation had reminded me of a traumatic event from my childhood and the memory was manifesting itself as pain in my knee.

After only one session I returned to physiotherapy and was able to get on an exercise bike. I regained the ability to walk soon after. I truly believe that if I had undergone traditional therapy, probably coupled with the antidepressants my doctor had been recommending, it would have taken many months before I recovered. Sandy's method is good at drawing out deeply suppressed feelings and dissolving them. I felt euphoric after my session, like a huge weight had been lifted from my head. I would recommend Mind Detox to anyone suffering from a physical condition that won't heal."

• • •

Meet Debbie, who had period pains:

"I had been suffering from period pains for 30 years, ever since I'd started my menstrual cycle at age 13. I experienced Sandy's method when I was 43 and wish I hadn't waited so long! Every month I was left with no energy and felt out of control and resentful. I discovered during my Mind Detox consultation that I had had my first period on my thirteenth birthday and it made me feel dirty, uncomfortable, sad, scared and unloved.

This emotionally linked with an earlier event when, aged four, I had felt the same in relation to whether my dad loved me. When I recognized the reality that he had loved me my whole life, all the other negative emotions cleared instantly. Two weeks later I had my first pain-free period in 30 years!"

• • •

TOP TIP **Saying the Unsayable**

One way to curb chronic pain is to heal events in your life when you've not been able to speak your mind or feel your feelings. By saying the *unsayable* and feeling the *unfeelable* once and for all – in relation to people or events in your past – stored emotional stress can be released, along with physical pain.

BENEFIT NO.2 **Loving the Skin You're In**

Skin is frequently one of the first physical signs of a person having unresolved emotional issues below the surface. The nature of the skin condition is often symbolic; by which I mean that skin hypersensitivity in the form of, for example, eczema can be the result of separation anxiety (whereby the skin is increasing its ability to "reach out and touch/find" the lost person, place, event or thing). Psoriasis, where the skin is producing extra cells, is often the result of an external attack, such as bullying or near-death experience, which causes the body to produce an extra-thick line of defence against the perceived threat.

As the human body grows a new skin by regenerating all its skin cells every month or so, healing can happen swiftly once the reason for the skin condition is resolved.

• • •

Meet Melissa, who had eczema:

> "I was a complete self-diagnosed stress-head until I
> met Sandy. I can confidently say that I am a much more
> relaxed person now and a number of the negative health
> side-effects of the stress have completely disappeared. I
> also benefited from the drastically improved appearance
> of my skin when I resolved the Root-Cause Reason for
> my eczema (which stemmed from an event that happened
> when I was a child). Now I feel brilliant!"

• • •

BENEFIT NO.3 **Brilliantly Working Bowels**

The brain and bowels are very much emotionally connected. Similarly to the skin, the bowels are prone to speaking the mind in rather symbolic ways. For instance, people finding certain events in their life "hard to digest" can end up with digestive problems. Those dealing with excessive stress or anxiety often end up with the additional concern of needing to find toilets quickly due to their chronic diarrhoea. People who have suffered loss in their life, are concerned about possible lack or find it difficult to let go are often more likely to become constipated as their bowels stop letting go, too.

• • •

Meet Tracey, who was constipated:

"I was totally stressed out, overweight, constipated, had oedema in my legs so bad that I couldn't kneel down, had no self-confidence and sweated uncontrollably if anyone spoke to me. I am now much more confident, 12 pounds lighter, with no oedema, no constipation and no sweating! Sandy's method is fantastic, and I can only thank you from the bottom of my heart – I am a new woman!"

• • •

Meet Ian, who was also constipated:

"I had suffered from badly working bowels ever since I was a child. I worked with Sandy when I was 34 and discovered that I had a hidden belief that it wasn't safe to go to the toilet. To be honest, once we healed that out-of-date belief I immediately had to go to the toilet as my constipation had ceased to exist! One month on and my bowels are functioning brilliantly, and I've even lost about a stone (6.4kgs) in weight, without dieting, now my body knows it's safe to let go!"

• • •

The implications of the mind–body connection are massive when it comes to understanding why people end up with chronic conditions, especially when no obvious physical reason can be found. This impact of the mind is especially important when you explore the extent to which your beliefs are not only known by the cells of your body but are also constantly causing physical changes to occur. More about this soon, but first…

LET'S PLAY A GAME

`GAME` **Mind–Body Monitoring**

For the next 24 hours, be vigilant about the physical reactions that occur in your body when you're thinking about different things, or when you're experiencing different situations. Notice what happens within your body when you:

- Think about certain memories;
- Think about someone you dislike compared to someone you love dearly;
- Think about different future scenarios that you are excited about compared to ones you're worried about;
- Find something funny and laugh;
- Find something sad and cry;
- Criticize someone/something;
- Praise and appreciate someone/something;
- Experience different external situations – like being stuck in traffic, being hugged or watching a movie.

A Vital First Step in Self-Healing

The first step in intentionally self-healing (I say intentionally, because you are unintentionally self-healing all the time!) is to notice first-hand, in your own personal life experience, that your thoughts and emotions *are* impacting on your body.

Becoming aware of this means you move from being oblivious to the ongoing, behind-the-scenes impact of the mind–body connection to a simple appreciation that it is happening. Although it may sound like a simple step, it is a leap towards taking charge of your physical destiny. Once you fully appreciate that your mind *is* having a real-time impact upon what happens within your body, it no longer makes any sense to solely treat physical symptoms. What *does* make sense is to adopt strategies for discovering and healing the often hidden mind-based causes.

CHAPTER TWO

The Belief Bond

· · · · · ·

HOW BELIEFS BECOME YOUR BODY

I CANNOT SLEEP. *I have underlying anxiety, but don't know why.* Have you ever had a creepy feeling that something bad is going to happen? I did, but I would have described it more as a deep-seated impending doom. The sickening sensation existed in the background, corroding my daytime calm and preventing me from sleeping soundly at night too; I felt an unexplainable uneasiness. But what I couldn't see at the time was how its cause stemmed from something that happened in my teenage years, which stole my innocent sense of safety in the world, put me in a constant state of stress and stained my perceptions of how I saw other people.

"What event in my life is the cause of my insomnia, the first event that, when resolved, will cause the problem to disappear. If I were to know, what age was I?" Age 15. "When I think of that time, what's the first person, place, event or thing that comes to mind?" I remembered the caravan site in Scotland where my family used to spend vacation time. More specifically, I remembered the pub that was located there, called Corkie's. From these clues the full memory came, which, until then, I'd rather have forgotten forever.

Early one evening I was inside Corkie's, standing at the bar ordering crisps and a Coke. To my left stood a man who I had never spoken to before, but I knew him as being one of the speed skiers on the nearby loch. He was a muscular guy, known as a bit of a joker, and had clearly been drinking. He turned to me and said, "I know what you did." I had no idea what he was talking about and told him so. Next thing he grabbed me by my ponytail (yes, I had long hair at the time, but don't let it distract you from the story), and with it firmly in his hand, he pulled my head down and pinned it to the side of the bar.

At first I thought it was just a bad joke but, looking up into his eyes, I saw he was clearly angry. I pretend-laughed, as the bar was busy and I wanted to maintain a brave face. "I really don't know what you are talking about," I said through a fake smile, with my heart pumping in my ears. "Don't lie to me," he growled. This made it even worse because I had no idea what I could say to get out of his hold and escape from his crippling grip.

What really stood out from the whole ordeal was that I remembered scanning around the pub, to see who was coming to save me, but nobody was. Everyone was just sat staring, with wry smiles, doing nothing. Eventually he released his grip and I ran out of the bar empty-handed.

To discover the Root-Cause Reason, I asked: "What was it about what happened that was a problem for me?" I felt *Petrified, powerless and unsafe with nobody there to protect me.* Up until that moment in the pub, however scary the situation, someone had always come to my rescue. This time was different, which is one of the reasons why it made such an impression on me, remained unresolved and created a toxic belief about being unsafe.

Having discovered the Root-Cause Reason, I then asked: "What can I know now that, if I had known it in the past, means I would have never felt this way in the first place?" I *was* safe, I survived and I didn't need anyone to help me. I now know that I have an inner self-protective strength that I can tap into if ever required. The other people in the pub didn't know how scared I felt inside, largely because I was pretending to be okay – it was natural nobody offered help. Looking back, I could also see that he was an unhappy man, which allowed for more compassion towards him. After installing these "knowings" the memory felt at peace, the Root-Cause Reason of "petrified, powerless and unsafe…" no longer felt true and, rolling forward in my mind, I knew I would respond differently if something similar ever happened in the future.

This past event was a defining moment for me, as life had never felt safe since. Consequently, my body didn't deem it safe to disengage my fight-flight-freeze stress response whenever I wanted to relax and sleep. I needed to stay alert to potential threats. Because of this belief of being unsafe, my unconscious mind would also constantly search for (and find) potential threats in my life, leading to chronic anxiety. Until I did Mind Detox, I was unaware of perceiving and experiencing the world as a dangerous place; all I knew were the surface-level symptoms of insomnia and unexplained uneasiness. Not any more! After resolving the memory and healing the toxic belief – "I'm unsafe" – the sense of impending doom dissolved and I no longer suffer from insomnia.

• • •

The Big Impact of Beliefs

Millions of people unintentionally hinder their health with hidden toxic beliefs that are harmful to their bodies and lives. These secret sources of tension put their bodies under copious amounts of unnoticed stress, which makes them more prone to experiencing physical "dis-ease". Beliefs also play an unseen role in many other well-being issues, for example insomnia, which is at epidemic levels, with a third of the UK population and around 60 million people in the USA currently unable to sleep (according to studies by the NHS and the American Sleep Association). Your beliefs are essentially the conclusions that you've come to during your life about your body, personality, capabilities, self-worth, lovability, safety and so on.

*Unhealthy beliefs can manifest physically as an
unhealthy body and an unhappy, unsuccessful life.*

Beliefs have been found to possess the power to influence many aspects of a person's physical functioning, including digestion, immune system, blood pressure and even DNA. Incredibly, beliefs communicate with the individual cells of the body, which can respond by creating physical conditions that mirror the consistent messages they receive from the mind. Our beliefs also influence how we interpret life events, thus impacting whether we experience a problematic or a peacefully productive life.

Consequences of the belief–body bond range from everyday physical responses to more life-threatening results; in a very real way, your beliefs become your biology. Recognizing the impact of your beliefs can increase confidence in your own self-healing capabilities. Here's some ways in which beliefs impact biology:

THE MIRACLE IN YOUR MOUTH… When you think about a food that you like your body gets ready to eat it. Your salivary glands go to work producing a fluid composed of water, mucus, proteins, mineral salts and amylase, an enzyme that breaks down starches. Amazingly, your body can react differently towards foods you like and foods you dislike.

When you think about a food you don't particularly like your body produces less saliva, making it more difficult to swallow the food you *believe* you don't like. I consider it to be one of evolution's smart ways to help us survive by making it harder to eat foods that may poison us. Two very different physical responses, yet the only way the body knows to respond differently is via the beliefs you have about the different foods.

CLOCKWORK ORANGE… Perhaps even more amazing are the experiences of some people with multiple-personality disorders. There are documented cases of the same person having different physical conditions depending on which personality is prominent at any given time. In one case, one personality was highly allergic to oranges and the other could eat them with no allergic reaction whatsoever. In another example, one personality needed glasses to see, whereas the other had perfect 20/20 vision. In both cases, the *cause* of the differences between the personalities existed in the mind and specifically the beliefs, not the body.

Placebo Power

More evidence of how our beliefs impact the body is the global phenomenon known as the placebo effect. This effect happens when, for example, a person takes a fake pill believing it is the real pill, but ends up getting better anyway. In the many thousands of documented cases worldwide, it is clearly the person's belief that the pill will work, not the ingredients of the fake pill, that causes physical healing to occur.

Just as powerful though is the harmful effect of the nocebo. The nocebo is the polar opposite of the placebo, whereby a person's beliefs play a role in them getting sick and, in some cases, even dying. I used to believe I would "catch a cold" a couple of times every winter and guess what, I did! Then one day I came across some compelling evidence that proved to me that it was actually impossible to catch a cold and, guess what, I've never caught one since. Is this a coincidence? I don't believe so. The placebo has been a powerful form of preventative medicine for me over the past few years.

On a more serious nocebo note, have you ever heard about people being told that they only have a finite time to live, say three months, and they've ended up dying three months to the day of the terminal diagnosis? Is this a coincidence? Again, I don't believe so. In one nocebo case I heard about, the person was misdiagnosed with a terminal condition and informed they only had a few weeks to live. They were then informed that their condition was actually treatable and not terminal, but died anyway – when they were originally told they would. I believe it was their belief in the first diagnosis that played a significant role in their premature death: a sad example of beliefs becoming the body.

Over the years, the placebo effect has split opinion. I urge you to never dismiss it as "just the placebo", which I often hear said. In reality, the placebo is by far the most researched form of "medicine" on the planet because every pharmaceutical drug has been tested against a placebo. The placebo effect is proven and there is much more evidence available proving its power to heal than for any other drug available on the market today. Meaning that your innate ability to heal – when doing something that you believe will cause healing – is very real and powerful.

Body Beliefs and Stress Beliefs

Having helped hundreds of people to change their beliefs, I've discovered two types of toxic beliefs that can impact the health: Body Beliefs are conclusions that you've come to about your body that end up becoming self-fulfilling prophecies. They influence the messages sent between the mind and body and directly impact physical functioning because the body follows the orders it is given by the mind. Some examples of Body Beliefs include: *I always feel tired at the same time of the day*; *My eyesight will worsen with age*; *I always get a nasty flu in winter;* or another common one: *I will gain weight with age.* This Body Belief actually caught me out...

Growing up I was constantly told that I could eat whatever I wanted but when I hit 30 years old I would need to be careful because I would get fat. Amazingly, within weeks of turning 30 I noticed my belly was now resting on my legs as I sat working at my laptop! I had gained weight despite my diet and exercise regime being the same as it had always been. I realized I must have picked up a Body Belief about gaining weight with age. So I set about doing what I could to change not my body, but my mind.

To help disprove the unhealthy Body Belief I set the goal of noticing all the people in my life who were older than 30 who had *not* gained weight. This helped me to heal the unhealthy belief because my mind now had lots of evidence to prove that it is possible, indeed normal and natural, to maintain a slim body the older I get. Within a few weeks my body was back to my normal weight and I could continue enjoying freedom with food.

BENEFIT NO. 4 **Life-Changing Weight Loss**

Although on this occasion I opted not to use Mind Detox – because my Body Belief had *not* come from an unresolved past event, but from the repetitive message I'd been fed growing up – excess weight is often a symptom of physical and/or emotional issues. Enjoying a healthy weight requires you to explore the reasons why your body has felt the need to adapt by gaining weight, and then make a few changes to the physical and emotional conditions in which your body exists. Doing so can cause your body to adapt again, but this time by losing surplus weight. Or if you know you are gaining weight because you are clearly overeating, then use Mind Detox to resolve the compulsion to consume so much.

• • •

Meet Susan, who struggled with her weight:

> "I had gained weight in my twenties, but didn't understand why. Whatever I did to lose it didn't make much difference. When working with Sandy I found a connection between when the weight gain happened and what had been going on in my life at the time.

It became clear to me that the extra weight was my body's way of protecting me from the conflict that was happening in my family. When I let go of the unresolved emotions relating to the difficult time in my life, I immediately began to lose weight. It was magic!"

• • •

Beliefs Stressing the Body Out of Balance

Stress Beliefs are the second type of beliefs I observe in people suffering from chronic conditions. These are the kind of beliefs that cause people to endure high levels of stress, unease and angst during daily life. *I'm not safe, I'm bad, I'm unloved, I'm not good enough* or *I'm abandoned* are just a few examples. Amongst other unhealthy side-effects, beliefs like these cause your mind to constantly search for potential threats, leading to your body being in a perpetual state of fight-flight-freeze survival mode and living in fear.

These beliefs also cause people to live with an underlying need to "run for their lives" through each and every day – over-working, over-performing, over-pleasing, over-compromising and overcompensating – all in an attempt to try to feel safe or prove their worth, lovability and enoughness. Stress Beliefs are so stressful because they justify a resistance of our current incarnation and daily reality, which as you will learn is the secret source of stress.

• • •

Meet Ros, who had chronic abdominal pain:

"I had been sent from one hospital department to the other over several years, but no one seemed to be able to discover the cause of my abdominal pain until I saw Sandy. He helped me to get to the real emotional root of the problem (which stemmed from the belief that I was abandoned) and the pain that had given me years of agony disappeared. All the other associated physical and emotional problems disappeared as well. Initially I was half waiting for them to return, but two years on I'm still feeling great!"

. . .

Ros is a fantastic example of how quickly the body can heal when you discover and resolve a toxic Stress Belief. Her belief was *I'm abandoned*. We discovered that she had formed that belief aged four, when she had managed to escape from her nursery and run home only to find an empty house. Her belief of being abandoned was causing her ongoing underlying feelings of hurt, which were manifesting as chronic physical pain. The fear of being abandoned again was also hurting her relationships due to jealousy that came from the fear of her husband leaving her. It was also compromising her career because she wanted to work for herself, but was instead working for a big pharmaceutical corporation. During our Mind Detox she shared that she worked there because she was "*scared of being out on her own*" – innocently describing what had happened age four!

Now, the truth is, she wasn't abandoned; in fact, *she'd* run away from nursery without telling anyone! But her belief that she was abandoned was enough to negatively impact her health and happiness for years. When she finally discovered the root cause of her pain and found peace with her past by remembering that her mum had come home and she wasn't abandoned but rather had run away, the negative emotion cleared, along with the physical pain.

One year after her Mind Detox we caught up for a lunch to celebrate her pain healing. She reported no reoccurrences of jealousy, plus she had taken the leap into self-employment. Ros's inspiring story illustrates the positive potential of resolving the root cause by purifying our perceptions about what we *think* happened in the past, which we'll explore more in Chapter 4.

Changing beliefs can cause big benefits within your body and life.

BENEFIT NO. 5 **No Sweat!**

Mind Detox has been successful in treating hyperhidrosis (over-sweating), which is often linked with anxiety and anger. In the majority of cases, the past memory is a time when lots of attention was on the person, which they didn't like for some reason and/or they didn't know what to do. This caused a shock, which the body has stored and which is why it continues to go into panic mode whenever similarly recognized events happen again. It is also common for the perspiring person to have felt unfairly treated, causing an undercurrent of anger.

• • •

Meet Alistair, who sweated excessively:

"Despite being a very fit and healthy Royal Marine, I had to hide the fact that I sweated uncontrollably. I had to always wear dark-coloured clothes, sleep on a towel and couldn't go for the promotion I wanted because sweating was seen as a sign of being unfit.

Sandy helped me get to parts of my mind I didn't know existed. We found a memory of a time at school when a teacher shouted at me unfairly and I felt angry that I was made to look stupid. When I achieved peace with the past event the excessive sweating that I'd had for years calmed down. I am now in control of the condition and able to get on with my life with greater confidence and peace of mind."

BENEFIT NO. 6 **No More Migraines**

• • •

Meet Sophie, who had migraines:

> "For years I had suffered with debilitating migraines. Working with Sandy helped me to find what had been 'on my mind' (albeit my unconscious mind!) the entire time. I was able to change the beliefs that were causing me to feel so negative towards myself, and clear the blocks that had been preventing me from making necessary changes to the way I'd been living life. I've not had a single migraine or headache since. My relationships with my friends have improved, and my fears around having a family of my own have disappeared. I'm now very happily married, and we are even expecting our first baby. Truly life-changing!"

• • •

Meet Rachel, who also had migraines:

> "I had been suffering from regular migraines for years. During my consultation with Sandy I discovered and healed the emotional cause of the migraines, which stemmed back to when a friend committed suicide. This also linked to an earlier event when a family member died suddenly. Amazingly, my headache went away immediately when I gave myself permission to be at peace with the passing of those I love. I've not had a migraine since."

• • •

BENEFIT NO. 7 **A Sweeter Life, Naturally**

I nearly fell of my chair when I heard about this success story from a Mind Detox practitioner working in Mexico.

• • •

Meet Rosa, who had diabetes:

> "I had severe diabetes and my blood count was 300 [unhealthily high]. The day after my Mind Detox consultation my blood count had dropped to 160! And now, three months after the consultation, my doctor has completely taken me off the medication."

• • •

TOP TIP **Befriend Your Beliefs**

Your mind wants to prove your beliefs right. So if, for example, you have a belief that you are abandoned, then your mind will do everything it can to help you be abandoned again and again! If you believe life is hard then life *will* be difficult. Or if you have the belief that you aren't safe, then your mind will help you find evidence that proves you're in danger. Not because your mind is against you; quite the opposite – your mind is trying to help you to be right!

Harnessing your self-healing capabilities requires you to befriend your beliefs by making sure they are working in your best interest. To discover Body or Stress Beliefs that may be impacting upon your wellness, it is useful to see the symbolic way that your body speaks your mind. Because as you do, you can discover that ...

Your Body is Not Against You

> *Symptoms most people consider to be physical problems can in fact be your body's best attempt at staying alive.*

Survival is the primary goal of the human body. It is not designed to just break, malfunction or get "sick" *without good reason*. Instead, every second of every day it is constantly doing everything in its power to adapt to, and survive, the inner and outer conditions it is experiencing. This happens because your body follows the orders given to it by your mind. More specifically, the individual cells that make up your body are so intelligent they are constantly adjusting themselves to the environment in which they *think* they exist.

Your body is programmed for survival and will do everything it can to stay alive. In fact, I'd suggest it is already doing so! What you may consider to be a physical problem is in fact your body's best attempt at adapting in order to survive the mental, emotional and environmental conditions that it is subjected to in daily life.

Adapting to the Chemical Climate

It works like this: your mind interprets whatever is happening in the external environment in thoughts and then your brain releases into the blood chemical messengers of your thoughts (neuropeptides), which tell the cells what adjustments they need to make in order to best survive the perceived environment. So, in the same way you would adapt to a change in the weather when it rains by putting a rain jacket on, your individual cells adapt to their chemical climate and the different chemical messengers they are being flooded with on a daily basis.

Your mind–body is communicating this way now. The millions of cells that make up your body are listening to your mind and responding accordingly. So if you are enjoying this book, your body is already benefiting! It also means that if you are, for example, being loving, your heart is quite literally experiencing love. If you feel unsupported, your knees know it physically. Or if you're feeling fear, your entire body is on physical red alert, with the fight-or-flight response potentially working overtime. Physical symptoms are often highly symbolic of issues at the mind level; the body does a brilliant job of speaking the mind.

It is the natural tendency of the body to heal itself,
and it will do so when given the chance.

Cast Your Mind Back

Remember Alistair, who suffered from excessive sweating? We discovered with Mind Detox that his sweat was, in his words, "anger bubbling up inside". When he let go of the pent-up anger, his body stopped the excessive sweating. Or Ian, whose constipation was the result of his body believing it wasn't safe to go to the toilet after a childhood "accident". His mind was trying to help by becoming constipated! There are more examples that spring to mind.

• • •

Meet Anna, who had psoriasis:

"My legs had been completely covered with psoriasis for over 25 years. I discovered, using Sandy's method, that it was my body's way of protecting me from a series of external threats, including bullying, that I had encountered during my teenage years. Within a few weeks of healing the fears associated with the past bullying, the skin on my legs was back to normal."

• • •

Meet Julie, who had lost her hearing:

"About 18 months ago I was diagnosed with Ménière's disease, a condition that affects the inner ear with excess fluid build-up, leading to debilitating attacks of severe vertigo, vomiting, tinnitus and eventually damage to the hearing, often causing complete hearing loss.

Gradually hearing in my right ear had deteriorated to the point of fluctuating between severe loss and moderate loss. I had needed to resort to getting a hearing aid fitted.

I attended the Mind Detox Method Practitioner training with Sandy in Australia. During the course Sandy demonstrated a one-on-one session with me in which I discovered a memory of my parents divorcing when I was six. I was scared at the time about not knowing what was going to happen, and I felt unloved. Sandy helped me recognize that life did go on and that I was loved.

After our session I kept forgetting to wear my hearing aid. I didn't think much of it until I was doing the meditation course with Sandy the following weekend and I could clearly hear a conversation on the other side of the room. At first I doubted it, as I could not normally hear a conversation that far away, even with my hearing aid. That night, to my surprise, I put my headphones in my right ear first and found I could hear! Normally it would be muffled but this time it was loud and clear. I had my hearing back and I sense the Ménière's has gone too! So perhaps what I needed to hear the most was that I'm loved! Thank you so much, Sandy, I'm now able to hear that I'm loved and so much more. I am forever grateful."

• • •

Also, meet Sandra, who had period pains for 20 years:

"Ever since I was a teenager I had suffered from intense cramps every month. I thought it was just something I had to grin and bear… until I heard about the Mind Detox Method. We discovered an event in my past where I had lost someone I loved dearly. When I resolved the resistance to letting go of that person, I immediately felt a release in my body. I have experienced hardly any period pain since."

Sandra was resisting the loss of someone she loved and her body was resisting letting go – through the physical manifestation of period pains. As you can see from these real-life examples, the human body is constantly adapting to survive in light of the climate of your mind. By changing your mind for the better, your body can change again, but this time by functioning in a more desirable way.

LET'S EXPLORE **Your Body Speaks Your Mind**

Consider how your body may be speaking your mind through the creation of a current physical condition. Just for now, let go of any medical labels you may have been given and, instead, explore the condition from a fresh perspective. Questions to consider are:

- **What is happening within my body, i.e. what is my body actually doing?** Is the body lacking *balance* or are your eyes not allowing you to *see up close* and if so, what in your life do you not want to look at or see?

- **How might the physical conditions be an attempt to adapt, be safe and/or survive my past or current life circumstances?** For example: Is the skin growing an extra-thick layer of defence? When you get a migraine, do you have a good excuse to hide in bed and stop doing stuff that you don't enjoy doing?

- **If the physical condition was trying to send a symbolic message to me, what might it be saying?** For example: If your knees cannot support you, where in your life do you feel unsupported or unable to support yourself?

- **If the physical condition was a negative emotion, what emotion would it be?** For example, does the toothache feel *angry* or does your irritable bowel syndrome feel *upset*? What are you angry about or what's made you feel upset?

- **How might my body be mirroring my life?** For example: Do I have a pain in my neck and if so, who in my life might it be?

- **Taking account of what's happened in my life, how might my body today be a physical manifestation of my past?** For example, does arthritis in your hands make it hard to hold on to stuff and does that reflect the fear of loss that has been a theme in your life?

- **What was happening in my life during the 12–18 months leading up to when I first noticed the physical condition?** For example: Were you scared of losing your job due to the threat of redundancies?

- **What bad things were happening?** For example: Were you going through a divorce or feeling super-stressed about moving home?

- **What good things were happening?** For example, did you finally finish a big project at work?

- **What problematic situation was resolved?** For example, did your divorce eventually come through or did you finally decide to resign?

• • •

The Good, the Bad and the Root Cause

You may notice that the final questions above ask about "good" things that were "resolved" during the 12–18 months before your symptoms first appeared. Although it may seem odd that a "good" event could lead to "bad" health, this can happen. On occasions like these, the physical symptoms have not emerged until *after* you disengaged the stress response by having some kind of resolution.

I actually experienced this when writing this book. I had been experiencing some writer's block (see the Preface for reasons) and when I finally had a big breakthrough I almost immediately developed a headache. Knowing that it was due to the resolution about writing, I knew what I needed to do Mind Detox on to heal it.

To use the method on such symptoms, consider what "bad" thing was going on pre-resolution (for me, with this book, it was concern over letting people down by not meeting my deadline). Then use Mind Detox to ensure the root cause is resolved. This can help the body to heal more quickly and not recreate the condition next time a similar "bad" thing occurs.

Overall, the collection of awareness-raising questions listed here will help you to explore whether there may be any possible mind-based causes for your chronic physical condition. If you think you've found a possible cause, take a note of it for later when you've learned the complete Mind Detox method. But before we get there, there are more things you need to know, to increase your chances of winning with this method.

CHAPTER THREE

The Resist Persist

· · · · · ·

HOW RESISTANCE RUINS LIVES

I CANNOT WIN. *Other people always achieve the success I want.* It didn't matter how hard I worked, success felt elusive and out of reach. A pipe dream at best, but with a very long pipe! Learning about the law of attraction and spiritual principles like "the outer reflects the inner", I became curious. Was my limited external success less about life being unkind or unfair, to me and more due to internal self-limiting beliefs that were pressing the pause button on my prosperity? I decided to do Mind Detox to find out.

"What event in my life is the cause of success feeling impossible for me, the first event that, when resolved, will cause the problem to disappear? If I were to know, what age was I?" I was four years old; Christmas time came to mind, which reminded me of the nativity play at my nursery. I wanted to be Joseph, but my friend Frasier also wanted to play the role and he was chosen for it. Using Step 3 of the method, I discovered that it was a problem for me because I felt: *"Sad and rejected because someone else was chosen instead of me."*

"What can I know now that, if I had known it in the past, I would have never felt that way in the first place?" It was not personal. There is a big difference between being rejected and not being chosen. The nursery teacher had to choose someone and, on that occasion, they chose another kid. Also, being selected to play Joseph in the nativity play had nothing to do with how successful I can be in life. I have the same potential for success as anyone, even if I don't always get what I think I want, when I think I should get it. With the help of Mind Detox I could see that my mind had taken that single event when someone else was chosen instead of me, and had generalized it out to form the belief: "Other people will get the success I want."

After I had taken on board these "knowings", the memory lost its negative emotional charge; I didn't feel sad or rejected any more. It no longer felt like other people would have the success I wanted because success need not be limited to a select few. Any sense of some external force deciding what was possible for me disappeared. I was empowered with the knowing that success wasn't out of reach; actually, success now felt inevitable. The belief "other people would get the success I want" no longer felt true and I also noticed that I'd lost the desire to overly compare myself with others. I'm not going to list all my successes since, but suffice to say the investment in doing Mind Detox most certainly paid off.

Saying that, I never want to give the impression that it is always as simple as **one** past *event* creating **one** toxic *belief* creating **one** *problem*. We are multifaceted human beings and sometimes multiple events and beliefs can be causing certain life issues, in what I call a Root-Cause Cluster. I will share another hidden cause that I resolved in relation to being more successful in Chapter 8.

Also, as a rather fun side note, let me share another quick story from the very same nativity play. In the end I was given the role of the innkeeper. I remember standing stage left, with all the parents sitting poised with cameras in hand, as I stood ready for my moment of fame. When instructed, I walked out and took up position behind the inn's door, which we had made a couple of days before out of old cardboard boxes and sticky-backed plastic. Mary and Joseph stood on the other side and, with a knock, followed by the words "Is there any room at the Inn?", I opened the door with such gusto that it came off in my very hands! I was left standing with the cardboard door flopping around by my side, and all of the parents bursting into laughter. I felt mortified. This was my first taste of being the centre of attention – and it was *not* good. Was it my most significant emotional event that led to my fear of public speaking later in life? No, but more about that later.

• • •

The Secret Source of Stress

Although short bouts of stress can actually boost immunity and raise levels of cancer-fighting molecules, being in a perpetual state of stress is a very different story. Your body ends up turning off long-term building-and-repair projects, and instead speeds up the aging process. Stress has also been found to weaken its immunity. Not only that, numerous scientific studies have now found evidence that firmly links negative emotions with the onset of arthritis, diabetes, heart disease, cancer and other problems.

According to Stanford University Medical School, the Centers for Disease Control and Prevention in Atlanta (CDC) and numerous health experts, the main cause of health problems on the planet is stress. Pointing to one very simple strategy for self-healing:

To increase health, we must reduce stress.

Here's an obvious yet profoundly important secret about stress that few people have ever stopped to consider: Stress is not caused by stress. Or, said slightly differently, stress is the result of something other than itself. Meaning that stress cannot be the ultimate cause of physical or emotional problems, due to the simple fact that there is something else causing stress. But what might that be? Resistance. In my observations, it is a person's preprogrammed resistance to certain life events that is the *real* source of stress. I say preprogrammed because our belief system plays a major role in what life events we resist or allow.

Resistance not only creates physical stress but is also *the* determining factor in whether a person feels negative emotions. Experiencing anger, sadness, fear, guilt or grief is only possible if you resist something in your past, present or future. Anger or sadness is usually the result of resisting something in your past, whereas resisting something bad happening in the future usually causes fear, angst or anxiety. Irrespective of the presenting emotion, resistance is the common denominator and underlying cause.

> *Resistance is the undercover cause of almost all pain, negative emotions and harmful forms of stress.*

What makes matters worse for the body is that most people prefer to not experience emotions that they deem negative, and so end up resisting not only life but their emotions too! I often see this causing a never-ending vicious circle of a person resisting more and more day by day, putting their body under ever-increasing pressure. No wonder this compounded stress often ends up with people experiencing physical disease, and so many of us are struggling with intense emotions, such as anxiety and panic attacks. Emotions are a powerful form of energy and if we respond to their existence with resistance, by perpetually pushing them down; they can bite back with a vengeance.

BENEFIT NO. 8 **Free from Anxiety**

The toxic beliefs associated with unresolved emotional events can put the body–mind into a perpetual state of fight-flight-freeze stress. This then makes us more inclined to constantly search our environment for potential threats, overthink and experience anxiety. We have also often been taught to resist the presence of any intense emotional energy that is considered to be "negative", which in reality only makes these energies stronger and even more intense. I will talk more about improving your relationship with such emotions in Chapter 10.

. . .

Meet Jill, who had debilitating anxiety:

> "I was getting daily bouts of anxiety. These were debilitating and stopped me doing ordinary everyday things. I would shake, feel sick, overeat to stop the nausea and rush about like a headless chicken, not really getting anywhere. Since using the methods taught by Sandy I have not had any anxiety, have much more energy and have been more focused and got more done. My life, and consequently the lives of those around me, has become calmer and happier. I laugh a lot more, and I'm sleeping better. Old behaviour patterns and past traumas are now a thing of the past, as I learn to live in and enjoy each moment."

. . .

The Resist Persist

Most therapy clients I meet are resisting something. If they weren't, there would be no reason for them to work with me because they would be feeling great and everything in their life would be okay! They are either resisting something that's happened in their past, resisting something in their present-day circumstances or resisting a potential worst-case scenario that might happen in their future. Using Mind Detox, I help them to find what they've been resisting and, over the course of the consultations, move them into a mindset that enables them to stop rejecting and start accepting reality. Guiding my clients to rise above resistance is my primary objective because I know if I can move them away from resistance, they will immediately feel better; this will help their body heal and allow their life to change for the better.

> *By rising above resistance you create the inner*
> *and outer space required for something new and*
> *improved to be created.*

What we resist will persist. Resistance requires us to focus on and think about what we *don't want* and, in doing so, keeps us connected to it. Put bluntly, resistance results in more of what you don't want. Rising above resistance, on the other hand, creates a space in which new and improved things can enter. By finding the subtle, often well-hidden resistances in your life and moving into a place of peace, you too can significantly reduce the amount of stress you endure. The less stress, the more healing can and will occur – not to mention, you will feel better too. Always remember, what you resist will persist, so if you also want to change your life circumstances, then cultivating a resistance-less mindset is a successful strategy.

Fortunately, it is never life events that cause you stress or make you feel sick, sad or bad, but rather your resistance to what's happened, is happening or might happen. This is wonderful news because it means that you can cultivate a choice. If you can learn to let go of resistance, you can massively reduce stress and negative emotions. They can be immediately replaced by feelings of inner peace, gratitude and contentment, which are, incidentally, emotions that have all been found to aid the healing process.

> *To resist reality is the equivalent of having a*
> *toddler tantrum because we aren't getting our*

*own way. If peace is what we want then we must
mature our mindset by not rejecting reality.*

But what if something bad is happening? Do you just accept
it? Yes, in a manner of speaking; but "accepting" it doesn't
mean you can't change it. It just means you don't cause yourself
unnecessary stress and suffering while you go about changing
whatever isn't acceptable to you. When less stressed and not
experiencing negative emotions you have more inner peace,
mental clarity and confidence. You also have more energy to
direct towards taking the action required. From this calmer
and clearer perspective, you are a very powerful and effective
person. You are able to choose to change your circumstances; the
difference if you've accepted things is that you can actually make
changes without having to experience any negative emotions to
justify your choices or actions. You simply choose for something
better while also welcoming whatever happens next.

So if you are currently experiencing a chronic condition or
persistent life problem, or often find yourself feeling negative
emotions such as anger, sadness, anxiety or loneliness, then
there is a very important question to ask yourself:

What in my life am I resisting?

Explore this question further by considering:

- Am I resisting the way I've been treated?
- Am I resisting the job that I do?
- Am I resisting my bank balance?
- Am I resisting my present physical health?
- Am I resisting how certain things in my life have
  turned out?

- Am I resisting something that's happened in the past?
- Am I resisting any areas of my life?

Answering these questions helps you to highlight the aspects of your life that you may currently be resisting. Remember, resistance is stressful for the body and the body heals best when it rests. Resistance also causes negative emotions, so peace comes from learning to resist life less. Resistance keeps you recreating the same life circumstances over and over again. So even if you want your life to change, it won't as long as you resist your current reality. Be super-attentive to what you might be resisting, and note what you discover so that you can rise above resistance for better health, peace of mind and happiness.

BENEFIT NO.9 **Enhanced Confidence**

I bet you're much more confident than you think! Are you confident making a cup of tea, cleaning the house or doing a hobby you love? Of course you are. This is because confidence is context-dependent. Meaning there is no such thing as an "unconfident person", only those who have habitual negative thoughts and emotions when faced with certain life events or circumstances.

Confidence is the natural way you feel when you are *not* thinking and feeling negatively.

People with confidence issues often worry about what other people think about them. So a key antidote to low confidence involves learning to not *need* to be liked by everyone. I offer ways to do this in Chapters 4, 9 and 10.

• • •

Meet Annette, who had low self-esteem:

> "I had so many issues to sort out that if I'd just got rid of
> one it would have been a bonus. I have found out, using

Sandy's method, that by getting to the root cause, all the related problems tumble away – and it works. It is magic. I used to think that I wasn't good enough, that everyone I love leaves me etc, but now, for the very first time in my whole life, I know I am perfect!!"

• • •

A Less Resistant Relationship With Life

What's important to appreciate about resistance is that it is often not intentional but the result of what's going on in the more subtle, hidden parts of your unconscious mind. Most people I meet are usually aware of the surface-level results of resistance, i.e. that they feel sad about the past, worried about the future or stressed about what's happening today; but they live unaware of the underlying reasons as to why they resist and end up feeling the way they do. Be easy on yourself as you move towards a less resistant relationship with life. The reason you resist usually exists in the hidden parts of your mind. This can make it hard to stop reacting with resistance – unless you know how and have access to a "peace-promoting" tool like Mind Detox.

Tune in to your mind by noticing your thoughts. The ones you can "hear" exist in what's called your conscious mind. However, there is also a level to your mind that operates below the surface of consciousness, which you are "unconscious" of. Working tirelessly behind the scenes, your unconscious mind performs many tasks without you having to be aware of any of them. It manages your memories, creates your emotions, drives your behaviours and is instrumental in healing your body. Understanding how the unconscious mind works and, more specifically, how it determines the degree to which you resist life, is vital.

Uncovering the Reasons for Resistance

Have you ever noticed how the exact same event can happen to two different people, whether that's giving a presentation or a flight being delayed, but one person will get very upset and stressed while the other takes it in their stride? Different responses to the exact same events are possible because we all have a unique version of reality. It works like this: You gather information about your environment via your five senses. At the point it reaches your brain and body it is raw data, without meaning – just light reflecting off the back of your eye to create images and vibration making your eardrum move to produce the appearance of sound.

Your unconscious mind then takes that raw data and makes meaning from the information by drawing on your internal filters, including your language, beliefs, values, past decisions, memories, significant emotional events and a few more. This unconscious process deletes, distorts and generalizes the data to create your unique version of reality – unique because you have a unique collection of internal filters. Helping your body heal and life improve by reducing resistance therefore requires you to change any filters that are causing you to reactively resist certain life events.

Discovering the Root-Cause Reason

By far the most impactful filter, which has the biggest impact on health, wealth and happiness, is that of your beliefs; they work silently behind the scenes, deciding whether you resist anything happening or experience peace as you encounter different life events.

Beliefs exist in the more unconscious realms of your mind, which can make them difficult to find and fix – unless you know how! To do exactly this, the method you are about to learn in Part Two first helps you to find what I refer to as the Root-Cause Event (RCE).

This is the significant emotional event in your life when you most likely first created the toxic belief. Events that are significant enough to create a belief usually have similar attributes: they are unexpected, emotional, are often isolative i.e. you felt alone or without the assistance you believed you needed and, at that point in your life, you had no pre-learned strategy to deal with whatever was happening. This combination makes them significant enough to create a lasting impression and, in turn, some kind of belief. Can you relate to the above factors? Any past memories come to mind? Take a note for later, in case you need to Mind Detox any of them.

As mentioned in the introduction, a toxic belief is any one that justifies resistance. So to discover what the toxic belief is, my method then goes on to find the Root-Cause Reason (RCR), which is a short sentence that summarizes perfectly why what happened was a problem for you. Therefore, RCR consists of the emotion(s) you felt at the time and the reasons why the Root-Cause Event made you feel that way. Make sense so far? Okay, let's continue.

Clarifying the Root-Cause Reason requires you to recognize that it is not *what* happened, but instead, *why* what happened was a problem for *you*: that is, the *real* problem. In other words, it is the meaning you attached to what happened, the emotions you felt as a result of your reactive resistance and the subsequent belief(s) that you formed (or already had) that determine whether or not something is a problem for you.

This is why the Root-Cause Reason, in most cases, is a short sentence that summarizes in a few words *why* what happened was a problem for you, usually consisting of one or more negative emotions and the main reason you felt or feel that way. Examples include: *Sad, scared and vulnerable when Dad left; angry made to look stupid; rejected when Mum preferred my brother* or *scared to see my mum so weak*. I have shared examples of Root-Cause Reasons in Appendix 2.

The Emotional Domino Effect

You cannot change what happened in your past, but you can change how you relate to what happened. Therefore, to heal your past, you do NOT heal *what* happened, but instead, *why* what happened was a problem for you: in other words, the Root-Cause Reason. Even better news is that if you focus on healing the Root-Cause Reason(s) justifying your toxic beliefs, you can sometimes heal multiple memories simultaneously.

> *By finding the theme that ties your problematic memories together you heal a lifetime of emotional baggage in minutes!*

Such a claim is possible due to the way the mind operates. Your unconscious mind helps you to recognize the people, places, events and things you encounter during your daily life. By asking, *Where have I seen/heard/smelt/felt/tasted this before?* and then searching your memories for similar experiences, you can make sense of whatever is happening in each moment. This happens so quickly we can easily take this unconscious mechanism for granted, but you can be sure it's happening if you recognize what's going on. For example, if you know you are seeing a car on the road, then your unconscious mind has made sense of the raw data it's received via your five senses and worked out it is a "car" on a "road".

To make its job easier, your mind links similar memories together. For instance, it connects memories about the same place or person. This is why when you hear a particular song it might remind you of a particular person, place or event, and before you know it you're taking a jaunt down memory lane. Or why things can be so emotionally difficult after a relationship break-up; everywhere you go and everything you do can end up reminding you of the very person you're trying to forget!

The great news is that, because your memories are linked together, you can now benefit from what I call the *emotional domino effect*. By clearing the emotion associated with one key memory (the Root-Cause Event), you can clear the emotions from all associated memories too – simultaneously! This makes it possible to clear a huge amount of emotional baggage in a very short amount of time.

> *The trick to the emotional domino effect is to find the common thread that ties your problematic past memories together.*

Exploring the Common Themes

Explore what theme(s) link the majority of your "bad" memories together. You can do the same with your life problems, too. In many cases, if you find the theme you will be well on your way to finding your hidden toxic beliefs. For example, you may discover that you always tend to feel "lost" or "lonely", or "abandoned" "not wanted", "alone" or "not loved" or "a failure", "let down" "unprotected" etc.

The theme often becomes an unhealthy belief – such as "I'm an unconfident person", or "I'm not loved" or "Nobody cares". Therefore, you want to focus on healing the theme of being "unconfident", for example. I've found that by resolving the reasons *why* a problem has existed, it has no alternative but to disappear.

BENEFIT NO.10   **Bad Behaviours, Be Gone**

Destructive behaviours such as phobias, addictions and compulsive disorders can be a thing of the past if you use the methods outlined in this book. This is because your beliefs determine your emotions and your emotions drive your actions and behaviours. By changing your emotionally fuelled beliefs, you more easily act how you want.

• • •

Meet Juliet, who was a compulsive cleaner:

"Everything had to be immaculate. I was missing out on going for walks and playing outside with my child because I couldn't stand dirt. Working with Sandy I discovered that I had made an unconscious connection between dirt and feelings of vulnerability. This meant any time I saw anything unclean I would immediately feel vulnerable and need to either clean it or run away from it.

When I resolved the cause for this unconscious connection I immediately became able to enjoy being around mud and all things messy! This has freed me up to enjoy family life more, which even includes the occasional pottery lesson!"

• • •

Meet Liz, who couldn't travel abroad:

"I had not been abroad on holiday for 20 years because I got really ill on the return flight from my last holiday and was convinced the same thing was going to happen again.

A few weeks before my holiday I spent a couple of hours with Sandy, and he helped me discover the real reasons why I was so frightened about getting ill when travelling. This not only helped me to enjoy the weeks leading up to my holidays without worry but also let me enjoy the flight without being ill and without having to take medication.

I now fly abroad and within the UK quite frequently and without incident and thoroughly enjoy it. My whole life has changed, as I use the techniques Sandy gave me whenever I feel stressed, and they work. I can't emphasize enough how beneficial it would be to anyone with any kind of issues, be they mental or physical, to spend some time with Sandy – it can change your life forever."

· · ·

Resist Life Less for Remarkable Results

Enjoying a healthy, wealthy and happy life is not some far-off fantasy. Instead, these ways of living are your birthright as a human being. Being well, accessing abundance and being peaceful and happy are your most natural ways to be because it actually takes the effort of resisting life to live in any other way.

Due to the indisputable fact that your beliefs impact on your body (because of the mind–body connection), your emotions (because they justify how you feel) and your life (because they determine your habits and behaviours), healing toxic beliefs can lead to big benefits. Especially now you know that a resistance-free life is a free life indeed.

And finally, remember: toxic beliefs are any that make you resist certain life events and by cleansing these beliefs you can discover that harmony heals and success is easier. In the next chapter I will share three reasons why changing your beliefs is easier than you may think, along with some enlightening life discoveries that my Mind Detox clients have used to purify their perceptions of life and, in doing so, experience peace, forgiveness and freedom.

CHAPTER FOUR

The Purified Mind

· · · · · ·

HOW TO RETURN TO REALITY

I CANNOT SPEAK. *I'm petrified of public presentations.* It has been said that people fear public speaking more than death. Until I did a Mind Detox on *my* fear of public speaking, I hated it too – and I mean, *hated* it! In the past, if I ever had to do a presentation at university or, later, for work, I would worry about it for weeks in advance. As soon as I heard the heart-sinking news of my need to present, it was as if a silent countdown clock had started and I became strapped to a conveyer belt of terror, like the ones in the James Bond movies, which ever so slowly would inch me towards my final fate. Thinking about standing in front of a group of people, with all eyes on me, would give rise to nausea-infused nerves. Fear would literally flood every area of my body and being. I simply couldn't continue with such a frequently triggered phobia and one that would stand in the way of my success.

Do you remember my nativity-play trauma with the faulty cardboard door of the inn? When sitting down to do a Mind Detox to discover and resolve the cause of my fear of public speaking, I assumed that this would definitely be the memory that would require some healing. However, it wasn't. Instead, I recalled a much more emotionally charged event that happened later, in primary school.

One day, when I was around eleven, I was in maths class. I couldn't do the long division we were doing that day and the teacher told me to go to her desk at the front of the room to get extra tutoring. After a few more failed attempts at helping me to "get it", she became so frustrated that she grabbed me by both arms and shook me. What was it about what happened that was a problem for me? I felt: *Scared and embarrassed, everyone is looking at me.* Interestingly, my fear and embarrassment didn't actually come from being shaken, but because everyone was watching me as it happened.

My unconscious mind had made the link between the feelings I felt that day and being in front of *any* group of onlookers. Then, fast-forward a few years, any time I was faced with the task of doing a presentation I would feel how I felt *then* – at age eleven in maths class. I didn't know that, of course. I just knew I hated public speaking and would aim to avoid it at all costs.

Looking back on the event, I considered the possibility that my fellow students were most likely thinking badly of the teacher, rather than me. They probably felt sorry for me due to what they were witnessing and glad that it wasn't them. I was determined to get peace with it and I knew I needed to move from fear and humiliation to forgiveness and freedom. I accepted that the teacher wasn't a scary ogre, but simply frustrated by her inability to be fully understood and do her job right. Although it wasn't pleasant to be shaken, it was only a momentary thing – nobody apart from me remembers it now – and ultimately I survived the entire experience physically unscathed. After installing these new-found "knowings" the past memory became emotionally neutral, the Root-Cause Reason stopped feeling true or charged and when I considered being in front of groups I now felt a combo of joy, excitement and exhilaration.

Since this Mind Detox, I now speak freely and without any fear in front of conference audiences of 1000+ people. I've even won awards for my public-speaking abilities.

. . .

Here One Minute, Gone the Next

Amongst other adventures, a large part of my life involves working with the members of my international online community (www.calmclan.com) and travelling the world helping people to heal by making peace with the past. Some have been experiencing extreme anger or sadness or fear for decades.

Others have resisted life so much and for so long that they have ended up with severe physical conditions. Irrespective though of how long difficult events have been a problem for them, there is always a point when they discover a way of perceiving the past that stops it being a problem. In doing so, they end up feeling more neutral or even positive towards life events that, for years, had been causing them intense negative feelings.

Witnessing this in literally hundreds of people led me to begin to question what problems actually are. I mean, if an event or experience is a problem for a person for years and then, after a shift in perspective, stops being a problem, was it ever a problem in the first place? Or was the *real* problem the person not yet being able to view the life event from a more positive and pure perspective?

Purifying Perceptions

One of my favourite quotes comes from Albert Einstein and goes: "No problem can be solved with the same level of consciousness that created it." I've observed that it is people's open-mindedness and level of consciousness that determines whether or not what happens in life is a problem. Not the event, but what they think *about* the event. One person might lose their job and be thrilled at the new possibilities; another might become physically ill from the stress. It's the same event, so what's different? They have differing perceptions.

Raising your consciousness to ever-increasing heights by bursting through your impure perceptions of reality is therefore a vital part of enjoying a more peaceful and positive life. It can lead to a liberated life free from problems whereby, although unplanned events may still arise, you don't experience them as being problems, nor as anything being ultimately wrong. How incredible is that? You don't need to wait for anything to change about your past, present or future to enjoy a more positive life.

> *When you purify your perceptions, life*
> *immediately improves!*

The Elephant in the Room

We are getting close to detoxing your mind of the possible root causes of your chronic condition(s) and persistent problems. But before we do, there is still some work to be done on cultivating the optimal mindset for more easily making the positive changes you want. As cleansing toxic beliefs is a core part of purifying your perceptions, let's continue by calling out the elephant in the room: namely the common misconception that it's hard to change beliefs.

> *The belief that it is hard to change beliefs is a*
> *belief that you can easily change!*

As you've already learned, beliefs play a key role in determining the health of your body and the quality of your life. However, whenever I used to sit down with clients and tell them we were going to change one of their unhealthy beliefs I would commonly see the whites of their eyes! This probably had a lot to do with the myth that states that it is hard to change beliefs. In my experience this simply isn't true; we are changing and making new beliefs all of the time.

What's Hiding in Your Closet?

I bet there is an item of clothing in your wardrobe that you bought a few years ago that, at the time, you *believed* made you look good. You strutted your stuff and felt fantastic wearing it. However, your tastes in clothing have changed so much that now someone would need to pay *you* to wear it! Fashion tastes changing is just one example of beliefs changing easily and naturally.

> *Beliefs are nothing more than conclusions you've come to at some point in your life, based upon the limited information you had available at the time.*

Wanting to help my clients to more easily make changes to their mind, I started referring to beliefs in a way that made the idea of changing them more palatable. These days I often call them conclusions. The good news is that, if you have come to some unhelpful ones, there are three reasons why they can be easy to heal:

REASON NO.1 Beliefs are Not Absolutely True

Truth is always true. Beliefs are only sometimes correct, in some circumstances, for a select few, in limited locations, at certain times. Truths, on the other hand, are always true, in all circumstances, for everyone, in all time and space.

The good news is that *all* beliefs are only relatively true. Any conclusion you have, such as, "It's hard to make money", may appear correct for you, but I can guarantee that someone else on the planet believes the exact opposite. So which belief is true? Both! But this makes either belief, only relatively true. Get the difference? Because beliefs are only relatively true, they are not fixed. Beliefs can change... easily!

> *You are not a victim of your belief system.*
> *You can change it if it isn't working for you —*

and I'd recommend that you do so if any of your beliefs are limiting your health, wealth, peace, love and happiness.

REASON NO. 2 **Beliefs are Fuelled by Fictions not Facts**

Consider this: how do you know something is true for you? Most people say, because a) it feels true, and b) I have evidence to prove it to be true. They'd be right; however, these criteria do not make their beliefs *absolutely* true.

One reason why people believe their beliefs for so long without questioning them is because they feel true. Usually because they've had events in the past that have "proven" them to be true. Beliefs feel true to you because they are supported by some kind of story from the past. Using Mind Detox, you will discover that the majority of your stories are mere fictions and most certainly not facts. They are based upon what you *thought* happened, rather than what happened in reality. But guess what happens when you explore new and improved ways of perceiving your past? Yes, that's right – they stop feeling so true and you naturally stop believing them as much, if at all.

REASON NO. 3 **Beliefs are Based Upon Limited Information**

Amazingly, you came to most of your core beliefs about yourself, other people and the world you live in by the age of six, a sprinkling more by age 12 and then only a few others since. Meaning you could have beliefs affecting your health when you're 40 that you came to when you were four! (Which is what I find with many people I meet.)

The younger you came to these conclusions the less life experience you had. No wonder your toxic beliefs are rarely correct! The good news is that, naturally, you know much more now than you did in the past. More importantly, with new information you can come to new conclusions any time you want. With this in mind, let's explore the most life-changing gems of information that my clients have needed to know in order to heal toxic beliefs and, in turn, enjoy the big benefits of resisting life less.

Is Peace Possible? Yes.

I love the question "Is it possible?" because it reminds us that even if we don't know how to achieve something yet, it doesn't mean we never can. Although you may have beliefs needing changed that feel very true to you, or some past events that you really don't know how you could ever get peace with, I invite you to remain open-minded to the idea that peace is possible. I promise that the more open you remain, the more peace becomes possible for you. It is never too late to have a happy and helpful childhood and you are about to learn a method that has helped countless people to heal deep-rooted beliefs and resolve really difficult life events.

I've been privileged to be present when literally hundreds of people have been resolving their biggest life problems by having their biggest life breakthroughs. I'm about to share ten of my favourite questions that have repeatedly helped my clients to find resolution. By answering them you can purify your perceptions of what's happened in your history. They challenge any assumptions, beliefs and attitudes that have been justifying resistance. I can't overestimate the power of these questions and the *home truths* that they hold at the heart of them. Knowing them now will help you massively when using Mind Detox in Part Two, and also improve how you relate to the rest of your life. They return you to the reality, where peace is patiently waiting.

• • •

Ten Questions for Coming to New Conclusions

Consider these questions and responses within the context of a past memory that you already know you are resisting. If you aren't aware of any possible Root-Cause Events yet, I invite you to be open to these positive possibilities being true, and refer to them in Part Two when using Mind Detox:

- *Were you safer than you thought?* Yes; the fact that I am here today to tell the tale means I survived.

- *Did life continue?* Yes; despite disliking the past moment, life moved on and there have been good times since.

- *Were they doing the best they could?* Yes; if given a choice they would want to experience peace or love, but they didn't know how to and acted in ways that hurt their own happiness too.

- *Were they dealing with their own stuff?* Yes; they were not enlightened and were blinded and governed by their beliefs.

- *Did you take it way too personally?* Yes; their unkind words or actions said much more about *them* than me.

- *Have you been mind-reading?* Yes, I've been assuming that I know what they were thinking, which I can't know for sure.

- *Can you honour them by being happy?* (For cases of grief) Yes; because they loved me, they would want me to be happy.

- *Are you more capable than you think?* Yes, I am a resourceful person, having always done what it takes to survive.

- *Were you looking outside for love?* Yes, and I now know I am a good and lovable person and don't need to seek reassurance.

- *Were you not being very loving either?* Yes, I could have been more unconditionally loving, judged them less and not forced them to be someone they weren't able to be then.

Let's dive deeper by exploring these questions in more detail.

POSSIBILITY NO. 1 **Were you safer than you thought?**

Consider this:

> *If you had known, for absolutely certain, that you were going to survive the past event, how differently would you have felt at the time?*

Feeling scared is often the result of our safety and survival being uncertain. When doing Mind Detox with clients to release past fears, they are often overlooking the undeniable fact that they survived and are still here today to tell the tale. Have a reassuring reality check now: for you to be reading this book means that you have successfully survived every single scary event in your entire life.

Obvious perhaps, but for many people it is a huge aha moment that they had never considered before. By recognizing this simple truth that cannot be denied, the mind is able to turn off the red alert switch and peace with the past is more easily possible.

Fear can be hard to clear if you believe staying scared is keeping you safe. It isn't! Prolonged fear is bad for your health.

Instead of dwelling on how scared or vulnerable you felt then, appreciate how resourceful and resilient you actually were, and are. After all, you survived! In acknowledging this, your mind will no longer be justified to chronically create anger or fear, and you will most likely experience a calming secureness now.

POSSIBILITY NO. 2   **Did life continue?**

When recalling the past it is all too common to dwell on the most traumatic parts. In doing so we often neglect what happened next. I appreciate that your memory might be about a tricky or painful event, to say the least. But I encourage you to cast your mind back to a point *after* the event when life had moved on; when you were safe again and things were better. Taking account of this additional information, your mind will be less justified to continue feeling bad.

Do you remember Juliet from the last chapter, who had a phobia of anything dirty and used the method to *clean up* her compulsive cleaning disorder? When using Mind Detox, she discovered that her Root-Cause Event was when she underwent a racial attack in a subway tunnel as she walked home from school. Her Root-Cause Reason was *"scared I'm going to die"* and when I enquired about what she remembered about the tunnel, she said there was dog dirt everywhere. I believe her mind had linked the feelings of fear with the dog dirt and over the years had generalized to make her feel uncomfortable around any form of dirt or mess.

When working to resolve the Root-Cause Reason I asked, what happened next? She recalled going home, having dinner with her family and watching some television. After taking this on board, when she thought back to the subway tunnel she felt calmer. Her mind had taken account of the fact that she would be okay and no longer felt as justified holding on to the old fear. This also undermined the belief that her life was under threat.

After the session she reported that the compulsion to over-clean had gone and she was now doing pottery lessons with her daughter; something she would've never considered doing before because of her avoidance of dirt. (You can find a video of Juliet's coaching experience with me on YouTube if you want to check it out.)

The Dreamer

A good friend of mine had been experiencing intense dreams that would cause him to lash out during sleep. When I asked him the questions from the method, we ended up working to resolve a memory of when his dad was having an angry outburst. I then simply asked: *What happened next?* He burst out laughing and said, *Well, nothing!* He reported having more deep and peaceful sleep from then on. I believe my friend realizing this allowed his mind to switch off "high-alert mode" – which was causing him to unconsciously resist rest – and let him enter deeper levels of sleep.

But what if something bad had actually happened due to his dad's anger? Taking account of what happened next would still help. I can almost guarantee that there has been a point since the traumatic time when you have become safe again. (Even if that time is right now as you read this page!) Focus on how safe you are *right now* rather than how you *were* in the past. Life has moved on; now is the time to remind your mind of *this* reality. Doing so can help your body–mind disengage panic mode and heal easier.

POSSIBILITY NO.3 Were they doing the best they could?

Within every human is the desire to be happy and to experience love. I've asked literally thousands of people what they want more than anything else in life. I've asked people with different financial circumstances, religious affiliations, ages and educations. Of these people, how many of them do you think wanted conflict, separation, anger, arguments or anything else negative? That's right, zero. Nobody. *Nada!* Every single person I've asked has wanted positive life experiences, such as peace, happiness and love.

Everyone wants positive life experiences,
including the people who act in self-destructive
or negative ways.

Blinded by Beliefs

I believe that, if given a *genuine* choice (i.e., if they were not being blinded or governed by their own toxic beliefs), anyone who has wronged you would always choose options that would move them towards greater happiness, peace and love – if they knew how.

Anyone who does not know how to be peaceful, happy or loving does not also need your criticism, anger or resentment; they need your understanding and kindness. For you to find peace you may need to be the *bigger*, more conscious person. (See Chapter 9 for more on how.) You do not need to agree with their actions, only to understand that, given their own toxic beliefs, they were doing their best. Remembering this helps you to perceive others from a much more gentle, understanding and compassionate perspective.

Is it also possible that *you* deserve the same treatment? Have you possibly been too hard on yourself? Have you forgotten that you sometimes have to make mistakes in order to learn what is right? Are you ignoring that you were younger then, doing your best and, at that point, also didn't know any better?

If you have been holding on to enduring shame or guilt, remember that at the time in your life you did what you did, you would not have done it unless you *believed* it was the best possible option available, given your set of circumstances at that time. There's no point looking back now, from a completely different time and set of circumstances, to judge or feel guilty about what you did in the past. You've since had many life experiences that have shaped you and that would cause you to act differently under similar circumstances today. Let the learning from it be enough and let go of any guilt.

POSSIBILITY NO. 4 **Were they dealing with their own stuff?**

This possibility is especially relevant if you've ever felt neglected, hurt, unloved, unwanted or let down by a parent when growing up. It provides greater understanding about the behind-the-scenes reality that was *really* going on.

As children we saw our parents as gods. They knew so much, were so strong and, as far as we were concerned, could do anything. It is only as we grew up to become adults too that we began to appreciate that they were *only* human and had their own limitations, difficulties, fears and emotional baggage to deal with. Furthermore, and at the risk of sounding crude, allow me to highlight an important point. Your parents had sex (or made love, if you prefer), and made a baby. In the moment of conception, they didn't suddenly heal *all* of their issues or become enlightened; they *only* became parents. Maybe it's time that we give them a break.

> *They shouldn't have known better because they couldn't have known better.*

By taking into consideration the challenging lives our parents (or other people) had, it is easier to understand why they left, or why they were moody sometimes, or why they found it hard to love us fully.

Quite remarkably, by acknowledging that other people have their own issues to deal with something magical happens – you stop taking it so personally how they behaved towards you. This in turn enables you to let go of any hurt, sadness, anger or feelings of being unloved or unwanted and move on, viewing them instead from a more understanding and loving perspective.

POSSIBILITY NO.5 **Did you take it way too personally?**

One of the most common reasons why people hold on to these negative emotions for years (or even decades) is that they believe the actions of other people have something to do with them. They don't! Their actions are their side of the fence. Your reaction to their actions is your side. Their unkindness, for example, is something they need to evolve beyond, whereas your need for them to be different is something you need to learn to let go of needing. Irrespective of the actions of others, it only hurts you when you take it too personally.

Everyone has a unique version of reality. Remember, it works like this: people gather information about their external world via the five senses. At the point it meets the mind it is raw data, without meaning, just light reflecting off the back of the eye to create pictures and eardrums vibrating to produce sound. The unconscious mind then makes meaning from the data by drawing on a unique set of filters, including our toxic beliefs. This process deletes and distorts the data received to create a unique internal version of reality.

> *Meaning not only do you see, hear and experience an edited unique version of reality; everyone else on this planet does too!*

Due to everyone having a unique version of reality, most people end up projecting their toxic beliefs outwards. Meaning other people do not necessarily see, hear or experience the *real* you, but only their *idea* of you, based upon *their* internal filters. Get the difference?

Believe it or not, this is great news when it comes to you being able to make peace with your past. It means that you have never (and I mean never) been left, rejected, hated or abandoned by anyone.

What your parents or peers or partners have not liked or rejected has only ever been their ideas about you – not you, just their idea, in their mind, based upon their beliefs. Your mum did not prefer your brother or sister; she only preferred the idea she had in her head about your sibling. Your dad didn't leave you; he left his idea of you, based upon his own issues, unconscious conditioning and unhealthy beliefs. Your ex didn't fall out of love with you; he or she came to dislike their idea of you, which was not, and is not, you.

Only an idea! It wasn't personal. What a relief.

POSSIBILITY NO.6   Have you been mind-reading?

I'm constantly amazed by the years of heartache people can go through, when all the time their justification for feeling bad is based on a mind-read. The reality is most people don't even know what's going on in their *own* mind, so how are you going to accurately predict the innermost thoughts of someone else?

Have you ever been cruel to someone you love? Have you ever pushed someone away who you actually wanted to be close to? Or said things in the heat of the moment, which you didn't really mean? If you've answered "yes" to any of these, then how can you know for certain that if someone shouted at you or wasn't there for you, it must mean they didn't love or care about you? You can't. So I recommend you set the intention to catch yourself any time you are making up mind-reads and remain open to a more positive reality.

Meet my dad, who hurt for half a century

My dad spent 50 years of his life feeling hurt because he believed his biological dad didn't love him. When he was very young, his dad left after returning from war, never to be seen again. Perhaps reasonably, he had assumed his dad didn't love him enough to stay and felt hurt by that "fact". Quite literally half a century later, when his stepdad was on his deathbed, he was told to "look everywhere" when clearing out the house.

Soon after his stepfather's death the unfortunate task of sorting through the house happened. As my dad was emptying the attic, he came across a book that turned out to be his baby annual, including photographs, poems and letters that had been sent and kept by his biological father. As he looked through the book, it became very clear that his biological dad had in fact loved him immensely. Furthermore, it dawned on him that his assumptions about why his dad had left had been wrong the entire time. Based upon a mind-read, he'd caused himself a lifetime of unnecessary hurt and heartache.

These days, my dad is one of the happiest people I know. For his sake, I wish he hadn't waited so long and I hope his story helps you to see beyond any mind-reads you may have made along the way. Similar to my dad, a very large percentage of my Mind Detox clients have needed my help to heal the belief *My parents didn't love me enough.* In almost all cases, the belief is based upon a mind-read. The person has been reading between the lines, assumed they knew what their parents were thinking and concluded the worst. Then, in a total turnaround in thinking, most people end up realizing that they were in fact loved, very much indeed.

In countless cases they recognize the parent (or whoever) simply didn't know *how* to express love in a way that made them feel loved. Which, I'm sure you will agree, is completely different to actually not being loved! For instance, if a child is left by a parent, it is common for the child to come to the conclusion that it means they are not loved or lovable. This simply is not the case. Coming to that conclusion is an assumption based on a mind-read.

See the best in the people who you think have done you wrong. You can never know what they were really thinking. Even if they did say hurtful things, how can you honestly know if they meant it? You can't! Everyone wants to know peace, love and happiness, so it is safe to assume whatever gives your body the best rest and your heart the most peace and happiness.

• • •

POSSIBILITY NO.7 **Can you honour them by being happy?**

Feelings of grief are common when losing someone you love. For many, it is a natural "human" response. However, if the grief continues too long it can eventually become harmful to the body.

People can get stuck in the cycle of grief if they attempt to maintain a connection with the person who's died by holding on to the grief, such that if they felt good again they would dishonour the person who died. An important question to ask yourself if you're experiencing grief is: *Would my loved one want me to experience long-term suffering due to their death?* It is safe to assume your loved one would never want you to suffer. You can honour them by being happy – as they would want you to be. If you remain unsure as to why your grieving continues, use Mind Detox to resolve the reasons and be at peace with their passing.

• • •

Meet Becci, who lost her best friend

> Becci is a Calmologist trained in Mind Detox and therefore already familiar with this possibility. A couple of years ago her best friend of seventeen years passed away unexpectedly. Naturally she was upset, as she loved her friend deeply. However, when she knew I was writing this book she wrote to me wanting to share how Mind Detox had helped her:

"Knowing he wouldn't want me to be sad, after a day of honest emotional expression, I knew it was time to release any resistance relating to his death and choose for a healthy happy future. Two years on, I am able to look back at that event and my life without him with a deep and lasting peace and with the knowing that whether he was here or not, he would always want me to be happy."

POSSIBILITY NO. 8 **Are you more capable than you think?**

When you were first born you needed your parents completely, to feed you, clean you and protect you. Despite needing your parents when you were very young, you are now at a stage in life when you can feed, clean and look after yourself. Correct? An obvious thing to say, perhaps, but for many it is a blind spot. Lots of people continue to hold on to negative emotions towards their parents for not being there for them when they were children. They hold on to the anger, sadness, hurt or fear the child felt – as if they *still* depend on their parents for their survival.

Now I appreciate that it might have been justifiable to feel these feelings as a child, but as an adult, the emotions are way past their use-by date!

Are you waiting for some kind of past support that will never come? Subtle ongoing resistance about how your parents were in the past can be destructive to your health, happiness and overall life success today. The resistance is caused by a part of you that is *still* looking to get something from your parents, even if you don't actually need it any more. Take a moment to fully acknowledge that you are all grown up. You are able to clothe, feed and look after yourself (even if you don't want to!). You can be safe and survive very well on your own.

Repeat after me...

I can look after myself, I don't need my parents any more and even though I might not agree with

*how they raised me, what they did worked well at
teaching me how to be self-sufficient, take care of
myself and be resourceful in this world. Good job,
parents!*

POSSIBILITY NO. 9 **Were you looking outside for love?**

Two of the most common toxic beliefs that Mind Detox
uncovers are *I'm not wanted and I'm not loved*. The subsequent
underlying feelings of being unwanted or unloved often lead
to a number of destructive behaviours, causing people to settle
for *less than* in relationships and over-perform in an attempt
to earn reassurance from others. These beliefs also put the
body under copious amounts of pressure and stress, which is
obviously harmful to health.

Consider this: *Are you waiting to feel wanted/loved by
others when you are not wanting/loving yourself first?* At
the heart of these beliefs of not being wanted or loved is an
unconscious external searching for (and "taking") of love.
Quite innocently, someone with these beliefs starts looking
outside his or her own heart to *get* love and determine their
levels of desirability, which end up founded upon externally
sought evidence.

*As long as you look for love outside, it will remain
out of reach.*

As long as you remain reliant on getting love from the outside
world, you leave the door open to disappointment. At the root
of this kind of externally found love is fear – because if love
is outside you it can be withheld or taken away. This kind of
externally found love is subject to the whims of others: this
means it relies on other people deciding if you are lovable
in *their* eyes, based upon *their* judgements and conditioned
criteria of what's *lovable*.

Relying on other people loving or wanting you to feel loved or wanted yourself is therefore a high-risk strategy to say the least! Often leading to much hurt and resentment and many let-downs. Even if other people *do* care about you, if you hold on to the toxic beliefs *I'm not wanted* or *I'm not loved* then your mind will often filter out all the love that, in reality, you actually do receive.

Healing this blind spot involves accepting the reality that there is nothing wrong with you, or lacking within you. That you can choose to love the skin you're in by appreciating the exquisite beauty of your uniqueness. And, most importantly, accepting that you are enough, exactly as you are now.

Accepting this enables you to find a love within yourself that is beyond the opinions of others and stops you being so concerned about whether you are wanted or loved by anyone in your past, present or future. (Please see Chapter 9: The Love Lesson for more on this important topic.)

POSSIBILITY NO. 10 **Were you not being very loving either?**

Mirroring the previous possibility, many people also hold on to hurt, sadness, rejection or resentment for years because someone didn't love them in the way they believe they *should* be loved. They feel fully justified, all this time, in remaining a victim to the other person not loving them enough, not being there for them, not being the parent they'd hoped for and so on. They almost fall off their chair when I ask them: *"Is it possible you were not being very loving either?"*

Love does not demand, it doesn't judge and it doesn't need anything to be different before it can be expressed. Love has no rules, conditions or requirements and does not have any hoops that need jumped through.

So if you have felt upset because someone couldn't love you in the way you wanted, ask:

*Is it possible that I was waiting to be loved
unconditionally, when at the same time I was not
loving the other person unconditionally? Did I
constantly want the other person to change? Was
I imposing my beliefs on the other person? Was I
being critical of their choices? Or was I resisting
who they are, instead of loving them as they are?*

Love lets everyone be enough, now, knowing that we are all doing our best and are in the process of learning how to love better. You don't have to agree with all of their actions. Just love them in the knowledge that they've temporarily forgotten that in their heart there is purity and goodness.

What Would Love Do?

One final powerful question to ask if you ever have a problem with a particular person is: *What would love do now?* Doing so often causes feelings of anger or resentment to fall away and be replaced with kindness, gentleness and understanding. You might be the very person in their life to show *them* how to love more unconditionally. Be the light that guides others home to the heart.

CHAPTER FIVE

The Safe Place

· · · · · ·

WHY THE PRESENT IS A PLACE OF PEACE

I CANNOT BE HERE. *The life I should be living is somewhere else.* It didn't matter if I was lying on a beach somewhere sunny, eating a delicious meal with dear friends or riding my motorbike through stunning scenery, I never felt fully happy where I was. It was as if there was a distance between life and me and I couldn't connect with true contentment.

It also didn't matter if I was doing something super-fun or more mundane, like shopping for groceries; I felt a perpetual pullback from wherever I was and felt I should be at home working, or somewhere else. Anywhere actually, other than where I happened to be and doing what I was doing. I would often say that I felt there was a party happening somewhere, but I wasn't invited. Can you relate to that feeling? When with other people, I would pretend to be happy. I would pretend to have a good time. But inside, I felt a separation and a sadness that I couldn't shake off. In short, I always felt I was missing out and that I should be somewhere else, doing something else. So much so that if I could just "get there", then I would finally find happiness. No longer willing to postpone my own positivity, I decided to do a Mind Detox.

"What event in my life is the cause of my constant sense of missing out, the first event that, when resolved, will cause the problem to disappear?. If I were to know, what age was I?" Age 16 came to mind. I was standing in the front room of my house. The space was dully lit and I was aimlessly looking out through the rain-spotted window onto the wet street outside. As the full memory returned I could still feel the silence of the room, an eerie empty quiet, filled with loneliness. I remembered that my *supposed* best mates were all together that night having a party and I wasn't invited. Recalling this memory obviously made complete sense, because it was exactly how I'd often described myself feeling, but had never known why, until I did Mind Detox that day.

"What was it about what happened that was a problem for me?" I felt: *"Sad, rejected and lonely because I am missing out on the party."* I recollected my parents coming and offering to do something with me. I reluctantly accepted their invitation, but for the entire time felt depressed at the thought of my friends having fun without me or not caring that I was absent.

"What can I know now, that, if I had known it in the past, I would have never felt sad, rejected and lonely in the first place?" Having been meditating for over a decade, and learning to embrace life, right now, as it is, I now know that I am always where I am supposed to be. I am sometimes invited and sometimes not, and that's okay. It's okay because I also don't always invite *all* of my mates to every event or party I host. They have the freedom to choose who they spend time with, and when, and so do I. Having been playing for years with being more present, I also know there is never nothing happening. That if I remain alert to the here and now, nothing is ever lacking and there is always abundance.

Finally, having since spoken to a friend who was at the party, I found out that I wasn't invited because one of my other mates liked a girl and he thought she might prefer me and therfore I was competition! So by not inviting me he was increasing the odds of her ending up with him. It wasn't personal – I had no control over if she liked me more than him and if I'm honest, as a teenager I might have done the exact same thing to my mate!

After using Mind Detox on this memory and resolving the Root-Cause Reason, the feeling that I was missing out dissolved and I was happier to be and do whatever I was being or doing. This Mind Detox has also made it easier to stay present and enjoy more completeness and contentment as a direct result.

. . .

So far you've discovered that to help your body heal and have a happier, more successful life, you need to stop resisting anything in your life – past, present and future. You also need to prioritize your peace and be willing to let go of anger, sadness, fear, guilt and anxiety, along with other downward-spiralling emotional experiences.

Thankfully, to enjoy more peace we don't need to become time travellers, able to change the past or future. We just need to learn to be more present.

The Power of Staying in the Present

Freedom from regular resistance and negative emotions is easier when you know and directly experience the benefits of perhaps one of the best-kept secrets in history. Namely, that *this* moment is the *only* moment that exists, and therefore, the only moment that is real. This one! No other. Not some past memory or future fantasy, only now.

Unfortunately, millions of people live their entire lives not recognizing this fundamental truth of life and reality. They go about their days replaying their past or pre-playing some future scenarios in their mind, as if what they are thinking about is real, again and again and again. In the process, they struggle and suffer from unnecessary stress and ill-health, simply because they are in their heads thinking about the past and future, missing the present moment.

When engaged in the act of thinking, you are more likely to use your sympathetic nervous system, enter the fight-flight-freeze mode and operate from your brainstem. The primary objective of that part of your brain is survival and as a result, your thinking becomes very black and white and fixated on potential threats and is more closed off to creative, calming and conscious ways of viewing life. This is, obviously, not the best state to be in when doing this kind of work.

Alternatively, when you are not thinking about the past or future and are attentive to "now", you are more likely to activate the parasympathetic nervous system. This in turn activates the relaxation response, which is proven to help healing.

Being present also makes it easier for you to do Mind Detox. The reason for this is that you experience what is referred to as the "waking state of trance", which is a supremely calm and clear way to be. In this state you have a less busy mind, the memories you need to remember are easier to access and change is more effortless. By not dwelling on the past or future and entering this supreme "present moment" state, you can also use the power of your mind–body connection in more productive and positive ways.

Your Body Doesn't Know the Difference

Numerous scientific studies have now discovered that, biochemically speaking, your body cannot tell the difference between what is happening in the real world and what is imagined in your mind. Meaning that even if you are only *thinking* about a stressful situation, your body still experiences the same negative physical reactions as it would if these events were *actually* happening in reality. Quite remarkable, I'm sure you'll agree!

The implications of these findings are hugely significant when it comes to experiencing inner peace and self-healing. Not only does it explain why so many people on the planet are experiencing physical conditions, it also validates the importance of learning how to think less about the past or future and be more present.

Products of My Overactive Imagination

Words cannot describe the relief that came to me the day I discovered that my memories from the past, irrespective of how bad or sad, are only accessible now via my imagination. The same went for all of my future fears. For years I would have literally been scared by my shadow, my imagination. Therapy to change or let go of my problems became so much easier once I knew that the past was nothing more than an imagined story in my mind.

When I was a child I snuck into the television room late one evening and watched the movie *Jaws*. It scared me to death! For weeks after seeing the movie I couldn't sleep; I was convinced the massive shark from the movie was hiding in my bedroom wardrobe, waiting for me to go to sleep before it came out to eat me! Now, looking back on it I can't help but laugh at the thought of a giant *fish* living in my wardrobe, but at the time it felt so real that I would sweat and shake from fear.

When my parents tried to tell me it wasn't real, it was just my imagination, I didn't believe them because it *felt* so real. But they spoke the truth, and gave me one of the most important lessons of my life. I've now discovered that my problems exist mainly in my mind, in either my imagined past or future, rarely in the real world of *this* moment. Please take a second to consider this possibility. Although the problems that cause you emotional stress may feel real, they exist more in your imagination than in reality.

Just because a problem feels real, it doesn't mean it exists in the reality of now.

Bitter Pill?

I appreciate this might be a bit hard to swallow at first, in particular if your problems feel real and appear to be happening now. But for the sake of your health and happiness, I invite you to notice that much of your stress and negative emotions are caused by thinking overly about the past and future.

Meet Mandy, who had been negatively impacted by past events for over 20 years:

> "I came to Sandy's retreat having been troubled by negative emotions relating to three problematic people for over 22 years. These memories had impacted my weight and I'd suffered from anger and depression. After my one-to-one with Sandy I felt unburdened, and completely relieved of all the pain I'd been carrying."

Mandy recognized during our mentoring that the things she considered problems today were not problems in reality, but only stories in her mind. She let go of 22 years of pain in a matter of minutes when she realized she was causing herself unnecessary stress by continuing to think about what had happened in her past. Once I showed her how to be more present she was able to recognize the difference between being present and being in her head dwelling on the past. That empowered her with the choice to either stay in the peace of the present moment or step into the pain of her past stories. She chose peace and I urge you to do the same. It also stopped her being a victim to a past she couldn't change.

The Peaceful Presence of the Present

Why is there more peace in the present moment? When you leave the moment to start thinking about the past or future, you almost immediately begin to feel whatever you are thinking about. If for example you are thinking about a sad past event then that is how you will feel. Or if you are dwelling on a time when you felt hurt, again, that is how you will end up feeling. However, if you give your undivided attention to the here and now, you immediately stop "feeling your thinking" and naturally experience more peace. Not because you are trying to feel peace, but because you are no longer doing anything that prevents you from experiencing the inner presence of peace, which is your most natural way of being.

> *Past memories are not the cause of negative*
> *emotions, but thinking about them is.*

Incidentally, this means that other people are not the cause of your negative emotions, either. Over the years I've observed a collectively held belief within the global population: "How I feel is *their* fault." Meaning: what someone else said or didn't say, or what they did or didn't do, are the cause of *my* lack of inner peace. This is the not the case. *Your* emotions are due to something that is going on within you, and not outside of you. A button has been pressed inside you. You are feeling what you are feeling because you are currently feeling your thinking. No button, no emotional reaction.

Now I appreciate if, for example, someone is *in your face*, then you may well feel something "negative" in these moments. I'm referring here to the rest of the time, when the moment has passed, but you are *still* feeling bad. If we eliminated the hurt, sadness, anger etc. brought on by thinking about the past or future, then we would experience a life-changing amount of peace during daily life.

Taking on board and applying this liberating possibility, we stop projecting impure perceptions of reality out onto others. We stop suffering unnecessarily due to the false belief that "I feel X because of them", and we can protect our peace by thinking less and living more in the now. (For more on this, please see Chapter 10.)

Stay In the Room

Mind Detox is a method for getting peace with past "stuff". Using it, you will purify unresolved past events, which in turn can help your body to heal and improve your life from now on. The reason for raising the importance of being present here is because remembering that no past memories are happening in the reality of now makes the method much easier and more comfortable.

The present moment is a safe place to hang out and "do the work" because whatever you are remembering isn't happening now. If you were actually with me, in a room at one of my retreats, for example, it would be very obvious that the person or event you are working on isn't happening *here*. In my room there is usually a comfortable seat, fresh drinking water, some plants, pictures on the walls, a window with a pleasant view and me smiling back at you, championing you to let go and be free from whatever has been a problem. In my room you aren't being left by anyone, hurt by anyone or, in the more sensitive cases, you are certainly not being abused by anyone. Stay *in the room* as you use Mind Detox.

By remembering that all you are ultimately doing is giving your imagination a spring-clean, by finding more positive ways of remembering the past, then the memories won't feel so real, daunting or personal. There is nothing to fear when working with the past because nothing you will be working on is ever happening *now*. The present moment is a supremely safe space to be. Even if a problematic past memory appears to be real, I promise you that it isn't. When doing Mind Detox, answering one of the questions is what *is* happening now. Everything else is nothing more than your imagination; similar to *Jaws* in my childhood wardrobe.

If feeling overwhelmed or upset, have a reality check. Notice what you can see, hear and physically touch – now.

TOP TIP **Your Life Circumstances Are Not Your Real Life**

One way of staying in the safe place of now is to recognize that there is a big difference between your *real life* and your *imagined life*. Your real life is whatever is happening right now and your imagined life is everything else. Yes, *everything* else! Now, to really get what I'm saying, you must be willing to see that, although it may appear that your life circumstances are happening now, they are not. Right now you are reading this book, for example. Everything beyond the immediate moment happens only in your mind and imagination. To remember and start thinking about any problem in your life you need to move your attention away from *this moment* to thoughts about the problem. The more you can remain attentive to your real life, the less of a big deal your imagined life is, ever.

The Makings of a Movie Classic

With Mind Detox you will notice that we don't dwell on what happened. Immediately after finding the Root-Cause Event, we turn our focus to clarifying and resolving the Root-Cause Reason. While progressing through the method, I encourage you to stay in the safe place of now and recall past memories as you would any entertaining story – let's say, from a great movie. Even if there are dramas, disappointments or cliffhangers in a movie, when recalling it you can enjoy it because deep down you know it is "just a story" and isn't happening in the reality of now. Actually, movies often have suspense, ups, downs, twists and turns; things don't always go to the characters' plan, but you stick with them until they come out victorious the other side. This is *your* chance to come out the other side and prosper over past events that may have gotten you down.

*It's time to start being entertained by your story,
rather than restrained by it. When faced with
plot twists, be present to access your superhero
potential and make it a happy ending.*

Healthy Mind, Healthy Body

By seeing your past as simply a story and remaining present you can significantly reduce harmful forms of stress – as you naturally resist life much less. You dwell less on the past and don't fight what's happening now or next. With fewer problems to think about, peace quickly returns to your mind. Due to the mind–body connection, the natural by-product of a peaceful mind is a resting body. A resting body is able to heal more effectively, enabling it to be in balance, function as it was meant to, age well and enjoy true vitality.

By letting go of the toxic beliefs, you can experience life as if there is nothing wrong. Life is perfect. You are perfect. Life is complete. You are complete. Life isn't broken, and neither are you. You rest in the knowledge that optimum health, peace of mind and happiness is your birthright, your most natural way to be. And what previously felt out of reach moves towards you by resisting less and focusing on fully embracing the present moment. It's a wonderful way to be. (For more guidance on being present and thinking less, check out my book *THUNK! How to Think Less for Serenity and Success.*)

$$\cdots$$

TOOL GAAWO

In order to bring your attention to the reality of the present moment and access the ideal state of being for making changes to your mind, I recommend that you use one of my favourite tools ever: GAAWO. This technique uses your eyes to activate your parasympathetic nervous system – by being Gently Alert with your Attention Wide Open (GAAWO). It is very easy, natural and it has worked for everyone (yes, everyone!) I have ever taught. Although the tool is simple, the analytical mind can interfere with it, so I recommend that you adhere to the following three golden rules – not just the first time, but every time you use GAAWO:

RULE NO.1 Play with GAAWO

When you were a child you played. You were curious, explored and didn't give up at the first hurdle. Growing into adulthood, we often forget how to play and get caught in the trap of trying to get it right first time. We can lose interest or give up, if we don't get the results we want or aren't immediately perfect at it. We can talk ourselves out of things before we even begin! For the best results, play with GAAWO. Follow the instructions, see what happens, jump higher than any judgements about it not working and keep GAAWO-ing until it's second nature.

RULE NO.2 Don't think about GAAWO

You cannot make GAAWO work by thinking yourself into it. If you are thinking about it then you will be in your mind and end up one step removed from the experience of being present (remember, whenever you are thinking you aren't present). Without the experience, you will quickly come to the conclusion that the technique doesn't work. It does. So be aware of the difference between thinking about GAAWO and engaging it.

RULE NO.3 You can never do GAAWO later

One common mind trap is the subtle planning to do it later. You can, for example, accidentally think about how you should engage GAAWO, or that you will do so after talking about a difficult memory or once you've found a solution to your problem. You can do GAAWO any time and anywhere and if you don't, there's a high chance you are postponing the benefits. Why wait, when you can be calm and comfortable now?

Are you happy with the rules? Let's get GAAWO-ing! Here's how you do it.

INSTRUCTIONS

STEP NO. 1 Look ahead at this page and, as you continue to read the words on the page, relax your gaze to let your field of vision spread out to the left and right. Do not look directly at anything to your left and right. Instead, use your peripheral vision simplyto notice what is there. What you can see may be blurred and not in sharp focus; that's okay. Your intention right now is gently to let your attention open up wide to the left and right as you continue to gaze ahead at the words on the page.

STEP NO. 2 Now notice what it is like to let your gaze open up wider, both upwards and downwards, again without looking up and down. In your peripheral vision you might be able to see your lap and the colour of the clothes you are wearing. Above you might see the ground beyond the book and/or the wall as it extends upwards to meet the ceiling, if you're inside somewhere. Irrespective of where you are or what you can see, gently let your attention open up more widely to notice both above and below simultaneously.

STEP NO. 3 Continuing to gaze ahead, now notice what it is like to let your attention open up wide to the left and right and above and below so that you are gently alert with your attention wide open. What's happening in your mind? Is it chaotically busy or calmer and quieter than before engaging GAAWO? Has your inner experience of this moment become more restful? Are you thinking about the past or the future, or are you present, noticing the here and now? Can you become aware of an inner spaciousness or even stillness, as you engage GAAWO now?

. . .

With a little practice you will be able to use GAAWO as you go about your day – when reading, out walking, chatting with friends, pretty much any time you want to feel centred and calm and be here now. When using it in conjunction with the Mind Detox Method, simply engage GAAWO as you progress through the method. This will help you avoid dropping into any emotionally charged memories and make the entire experience more comfortable, even if you happen to be working on memories that you've previously found problematic. I promise, if you can remain in the safe place of the present, not just when doing Mind Detox but any time you remember to be so, then every moment can be an enjoyable one.

*"As my heart opened
I gained a simmering affection for others
and life."*

DAVID R. HAMILTON, PHD

PART TWO

The Method

· · · · · ·

DISCOVER AND RESOLVE
THE ROOT CAUSES OF CHRONIC CONDITIONS
AND PERSISTENT PROBLEMS

I Highly Recommend You...

Prepare Properly

I've written this book in a special order to ensure the greatest success. Don't jump to this point in the book. Make sure you read chapters 1–5 and also take on board the 8 Prep Steps shared from page 119 onwards, before attempting to use the 5-Step Mind Detox Method on a problem.

Please do not use this method on your own without the guidance of a trained Mind Detox practitioner or Calmologist if you believe there is a chance you could come across a past event that you would not want to work on by yourself. If in doubt, please see my website (*www.sandynewbigging.com*) to book some one-to-one mentoring with me. International consultations are available via Skype.

No Problem?

If you have no physical, emotional and life problems right now, then read through the list of Top 20 Toxic Beliefs in Appendix 2 (page 203) to check if you have any toxic beliefs that could cause you problems in the future. If none of these unhealthy beliefs feel true, then great! Check out the "My Incorrect Conclusions" tool in Chapter 8 to find any beliefs that you may have that are not working for you, and use the method to find when you formed the unhelpful toxic belief and cleanse it, for good.

CHAPTER SIX

The Mind Detox Method

· · · · · ·

DISCOVER AND RESOLVE YOUR ROOT CAUSES

I HATE NEGATIVITY. *I am triggered by and want to run away from anything negative, especially negative people acting like victims.* The day before sitting down to write this chapter I had a Mind Detox mentoring session scheduled with a client called James. As it was such a clear demonstration of the power of this method in action, let's start by sharing the story of how the session went.

James wanted my help because he'd noticed that any time he was around any form of negativity whatsoever he quickly became emotionally triggered. He would resist it, becoming angry as a result, had zero tolerance of anyone "playing the victim" and found himself feeling the need to run away from anything negative. This was especially tricky as he admitted that his number one negativity trigger was his mum! He didn't want to avoid her, but instead, wanted to be a more caring and compassionate person in general. We used Mind Detox to find the potential cause of his unwanted emotional reactions and resolve them, for good.

I asked him: "What event in your life is the cause of resisting negativity, the first event that, when resolved, will cause the problem to disappear? If you were to know, what age were you?" Age six was what came to James' mind. "When you think about that time, what's the first person, place, event or thing that comes to mind?" James remembered being in the family room at home, where his parents were arguing.

"What was it about watching your parents argue that was a problem for you?" I asked. The answer was, "It made me feel scared, insecure and unsafe." Sensing that there were more emotions going on for James, I asked: "How else did it make you feel?" He remembered feeling confused because he didn't understand why people didn't live in peace. We moved on to clarify the rest of the Root-Cause Reason: "Ultimately, what was it about what happened that made you feel scared, confused, insecure and unsafe?" James shared that he felt that way because he hated to see his parents unhappy. Combining this with what we had already discovered, we now had a complete Root-Cause Reason: *Scared, confused, insecure and unsafe when I see my parents unhappy*" and this reason for why it was a problem for James rated a 10/10 of emotional intensity.

"What can you know now that, if you had known it in the past, would have meant you would have never felt that way in the first place?" James said he now knew that he was okay, he was loved, physically fine the entire time and that ultimately he survived the whole thing. He went on to share how he now knows people fight sometimes, but despite this, life continues. He also lightened up when saying his mum is an Italian New Yorker with a fiery personality, so seeing her upset sometimes is kind of expected and isn't the end of the world. We then used the Install the Knowing exercise (see page 132) to install these new ways of viewing the past event into his body–mind and retested the intensity of the Root-Cause Reason, which now rated at 1/10.

Aiming to get the score to a zero, I asked: "Is it possible for you to be at peace with seeing your parents unhappy, at some point in your life?" Through a hopeful smile, James said "Yes, it's possible". I invited him to go into the future and imagine "stepping into" the older version of himself who is already over it. "What does the future you know, in order to be at peace with it then?" James responded: "I know peace is a choice and ultimately, I am peace." Immediately, a big smile came over his face and I could see a major shift occur in front of my eyes. James was positively glowing! After installing the additional learning, his Root-Cause Reason scored 0/10, the memory was emotionally neutral and he knew deeply that if ever faced with negativity in the future, he wouldn't recoil from it or resist it, and instead would just do or say what he could in order to help the other people know peace is a choice for them too.

Before doing Mind Detox, James didn't know peace was a choice and so he was highly protective of his peace. He felt threatened that if he ever left his peace, by being taken away from it by any external negativity, he might not be able to make his way back. This is what he was living unconsciously scared of, but when he embodied that peace is a choice, negativity was no longer something to fear.

. . .

Overview of 5-Step Mind Detox Method

Now that you've read the stories I've shared so far on how I've personally used Mind Detox, and the stories of working with my clients, it is my hope that the method is already feeling familiar. Having also read about the positive "knowings" used for purifying perceptions, you may also already be noticing some inner shifts, as your mind naturally takes them on board in relation to your own life.

Mind Detox discovers and resolves the undercover root cause by finding the Root-Cause Event, clarifying the Root-Cause Reason and then resolving it by considering more positive ways of recalling the past event. The method consists of five steps:

STEP NO.1 **When Did It Start?**

Finds the age of the Root-Cause Event.

STEP NO.2 **What Happened?**

Helps you to recall the memory of what happened.

STEP NO.3 **Why Was It a Problem?**

Explores why what happened was a problem for you so you can define the Root-Cause Reason.

STEP NO.4 **Why Not a Problem Now?**

Considers what you know now to be at peace with the past.

STEP NO.5 **Test the Work**

Checks the emotional rating of the past memory and Root Cause Reason. If both feel neutral and you would respond more positively to a similar event in the future, then the toxic belief is healed.

• • •

8 Prep steps for the best results

Get ready for results. Equally as important as the method itself is the state that you are in when doing the work. The first five chapters are intended to provide the general background theory and mindset required for understanding why a method like this works so well. But if you attempt to do Mind Detox without being in the right frame of mind, it can be tricky. To help you, here are 8 final prep steps that I encourage you to follow:

PREP STEP NO.1 **Be Innocent**

The chances are you've read other "health" books and this isn't your first attempt at healing a physical condition, emotional issue or life problem. People using my method have often tried other approaches, sometimes without success. Irrespective of what's happened in the past, I invite you to step forward with fresh eyes, an open mind and as much belief as possible in this working for you. Trust the process, suspend judgement and jump in with as much childlike curiosity and innocence as you can muster. Leave doubt at the door when using Mind Detox and do your best to not let scepticism steal your success.

PREP STEP NO.2 Be Willing to Change

Although, in reality, most people's comfort zones are pretty uncomfortable, self-limiting beliefs, health problems and problems can become familiar. And with familiarity, there can come a sense of security. Be honest with yourself when considering:

- Are you willing to draw a line in the sand and step out into perhaps unfamiliar territory?

- Are you willing to do things differently?

- Are you willing to trust the process, even if at the start some parts may seem pointless?

If the answer to all of these is "yes", then you are reading the right book and using the right technique for you.

PREP STEP NO.3 Be Beyond Your Story

Sometimes we can be so close to our life that we can't see the wood for the trees. Or, in other words, we can get so lost in our personal story that we don't actually know what we need to work on. At the beginning of every Mind Detox consultation I allow time and space for my clients to share their story of what they see as the wrongs and rights of whatever is happening in their life. But – without wanting to sound rude – I don't focus on the story! Instead, I listen beyond the words so that I am better able to offer clarity on what we actually need to work on.

To do this I remember:

In life, you either get the results you want or the reasons why you're not getting what you want.

Mind Detox works to clear the reasons why you haven't been getting the results you want. Reasons usually include ill-health, negative emotions and unhelpful habits. With this in mind, consider this: What do you want to let go of? Do you want to:

- Heal a physical condition
- Clear emotional baggage (including anger, sadness, fear, guilt, hurt, grief and anxiety)?
- Stop creating a particular negative life situation?
- Is there anything else specific you want to work on?

Note your reasons for using Mind Detox under these main categories now. Focus on what you want to let go of, rather than on *all the reasons* why you may believe it's going to be hard to heal. You may find it is easier than you think!

PREP STEP NO.4 **Be Clear on the Results You Want**

For you to get the results you want, it is vital that you begin with a clear positive intention. Again, to keep things simple, you can categorize your results under two main headings: states and outcomes. States that you may want to focus on creating are:

- happiness
- peace
- love
- confidence
- contentment

The great news with states is that the ingredients for any positive state you want are already residing within you, which means that it need not take much time to enjoy the states you want. Outcomes, on the other hand, can sometimes take time to create. Do you want to meet a loving life partner, start your own business or be slimmer? When considering the outcomes you want, it is very important that you are super-clear on how you will know when you've achieved your goal. Doing this will give you a fixed future moment when you will know that Mind Detox has done its work.

PREP STEP NO.5 Be Easy On Yourself

Reading a book like this one can make you more aware of how your thoughts, emotions and lifestyle may be negatively impacting on your physical health. But what's very important to keep in mind is that, although your health, wealth and happiness – or lack of them – are your responsibility, you have not intentionally done it to yourself and it is not your fault. The ultimate cause of your thinking patterns, emotional habits and behaviours exists in the more subtle realms of your mind; therefore, blaming yourself or feeling guilty about what's happening to your body or life does not help you to heal. Quite the opposite, in fact. Be easy on yourself and gently make whatever positive changes you can, at a pace that is comfortable for you.

PREP STEP NO.6 Be the Genius You Already Are

You may not think it but you are an absolute genius! Whenever I sit in front of clients at a clinic or retreat I make sure that I look to see the genius within. I assume that every person I meet knows the answer to *every* question that I'm going to ask them (especially when they think they don't!) and fully expect them to be able to make any inner change that is involved in their healing.

The magical thing is that when I see the genius in others, they begin to see it within themselves. There is no doubt in *my* mind that you can do it; you should think the same of yourself.

PREP STEP NO.7 Be a Miracle-Maker

All things are possible. I'm not sure where I picked up this belief, but I have noticed that it is a key ingredient to doing the Mind Detox work. Without living with the possibility that all things are possible, I would have probably turned away 95 per cent of the people I've successfully worked with. I would have never attempted to help the first person who walked through my door with a skin condition or digestive disorder, or was convinced that they were depressed. I would have bought in to the limiting belief that these were physical conditions and mind-based therapeutic work could not help.

Thankfully, my open-mindedness to the idea that all things are possible gave me permission to "give it a go" and see what happened. I invite you now to trust your miraculous body and the wise universe to take care of the details. Your job is simply to be open to the possibility and proceed with optimism.

PREP STEP NO.8 Be Committed

Do you really want to heal and/or experience life differently? Are you willing to persist until you succeed? People who have had complete remissions from illnesses or transformed their lives for the better have made it their number one priority, for as long as it has taken. You may need to use Mind Detox multiple times on the same issue, as there could be what I call a Root-Cause Cluster. This is when there are multiple Root-Cause Events or Reasons causing a particular issue. In my experience, Mind Detox works if you don't give up too soon. Don't try it to see if it works; instead, do it until it does.

Commitment makes the realization of your desired results inevitable because instead of focusing on whether you will do it, you focus your attention on why you want it and what you can actively do to get it. I certainly didn't do it in a day, and I continue to practise too. Decide now to do what it takes and do not stop until you succeed. There is an old Chinese proverb:

*Man who tries to cross a river in more than one
boat is bound to find himself getting wet.*

I love this quote because it summarizes so perfectly the need for being one-pointed. Your mind, body and the universe respond quickest if you proceed with one-pointedness, which essentially means to take action without tentativeness and distractions and with determination. Whether you only need to do one or multiple Mind Detoxes, by being committed with a one-pointed focus on your objectives, you can massively improve your chances of success.

. . .

The 5-Step Mind Detox Method

Let's work through the 5-Step method now.

STEP NO.1 **When Did It Start?**

(Find Root-Cause Event) Choose the physical condition, emotional issue or life problem that you would like to heal. With your permission, let's find out when this problem started so that you can move on and stop it being a problem now. Trust your first answer to these questions:

> **ASK: What event in my life is the cause of (state problem here), the first event that, when resolved, will cause the problem to disappear? If I were to know, what age was I? (e.g., "What event in my life is the cause of the psoriasis/ anxiety/migraines, the first event that, when resolved...")**

TOP TIP **Avoid editing your first thoughts or disregarding your immediate answer if it is not what you expected.**

In most cases, the Root-Cause Event happened before you were ten, so trust and go with your first answer.

From an initial sea of infinite possibilities, the answer to this question narrows your investigations down to a specific moment in time, like you at age two, six or 16. This will help your mind to uncover the memory of the possible Root-Cause Event now. Once you have discovered an age, it's time to move on to...

STEP NO. 2 **What Happened?**

(Clarify the Memory) Let's learn more about what happened at the age you've found, so that you can establish the Root-Cause Event that was a problem for you.

You will do this by clarifying the content: the specific person(s), place, event(s) or thing(s) that were involved.

Hold the age you found in Step 1 in your mind while you discover, and trust, your first answers to the following question:

> **ASK: When I think of that time, what is the first person, place, event or thing to come to mind now?**

Examples of possible answers include:

- The first *person*:
  "Dad", "Mum", "Grandfather", "schoolteacher", "brother","best friend".

- The first *place*:
  "home", "kitchen", "bedroom", "the park near my house", "nursery/school".

- The first *event*:
  "an argument", "first day of school", "getting lost", "being shouted at", "someone leaving", "wrong answer".

- The first *thing*:
  "my teddy", "Grandmother's perfume", "being cold", "being scared", "box of matches", or any object (an obvious one or a symbolic one) your mind is giving you to help you remember the entire memory.

Remembering the Memory Now

You may by now have recalled a specific detailed memory. If not, then you should focus on remaining open-minded and curious about what might have happened around that time in your life. It can feel as if you are making it up; that's common. You may need to dig around a bit before the complete memory returns to you. In the same way a detective would ask questions to find out what happened, you might want to also ask:

When I think of this (person, place, etc.), what else comes to mind? Who was there? Where was I? What might have happened in relation to (person, place, etc.) around that time in my life?

For example, if your answer to Step 1 was "age four" and your first answer to Step 2 was "Dad", then ask, *When I think about age four and my dad, what else comes to mind?* Or, if your first answer was "box of matches", then ask: *When I think of age four and a box of matches, who or where pops into my mind now? Who else might have been there? What else was going on?*

Like an artist painting a picture, aim to gather as many details as you need to paint an accurate picture of what might have happened. Your goal is to find a memory of an event that could have been a problem for you then. The moment you find a problematic memory immediately go to Step 3 (page 128).

Struggling to Find a Memory? Ask Yourself:

- When in my life did I not have this problem?
- When did I first notice I had this problem?
- How long have I had this problem?
- What was happening during the 12 to 18 months leading up to the first time I noticed the problem?

These questions can give you clues as to the possible Root-Cause Event. For instance, I once asked a client who'd been suffering from migraines, *When did you first notice you had migraines?* She remembered that she'd got her first migraine around the time a friend committed suicide. This then reminded her of an older memory, from when she was 12, when her aunt died suddenly. We worked on healing the age-12 memory, and once we had, she stopped getting migraines.

Still Not Found a Memory? Don't Worry, Try This:

Create an emotional-events tracker. In a journal, write down, in age order, all the significant emotional events of your life thus far. For example:

- **AGE FOUR:** Scared leaving Mum at the school gates.
- **AGE SEVEN:** Sad when best friend moved away.
- **AGE EIGHT:** Scared when lost at the supermarket.
- **AGE TWELVE:** Hurt not invited to friend's party.

And so on. Keep exploring what might have happened until you find a specific event that could have been a problem for you. If you find this impossible, then work on a more recent memory that comes to mind when you think about the physical condition, emotional issue or life problem. Once you have found a problematic memory, you are ready to progress on to...

STEP NO.3 Why Was It a Problem?

(Find Root-Cause Reason) Without a time machine, you cannot change what has happened in your past. However, the great news is you don't have to. You can change your *relationship* with what happened. To do this we don't work on *what* happened, but instead, we focus on *why* what happened was a problem for you then. This is a much more effective way to heal past memories because when you heal the reason *why* it was a problem, there is no reason for it be a problem any more.

Find the Root-Cause Reason

The Root-Cause Reason (RCR) is the reason *why* what happened was a problem for you. To discover it you need to explore how you interpreted the past events at the time, the subsequent emotions you felt and the possible conclusions you came to in light of the emotional events that happened.

Bring to mind the Root-Cause Event you discovered in Steps 1 and 2, so that you can now discover the RCR:

> **FOR EMOTIONS, ASK: What is it about what happened that was a problem for me? How did it make me feel?**
>
> **Ask yourself the above questions until you get one or more negative emotions. Then:**
>
> **FOR REASONS, ASK: Ultimately, what was it about what happened that caused me to feel that way?**

Keep It Simple

Don't overcomplicate this part of the method. You simply want to consider why you felt the way you did, so you can find the biggest reason for why you felt bad at that moment in your life. Aim to state the Root-Cause Reason in uncomplicated, simple words. Remember that you probably came to the conclusion when you were very young. It can help to include the emotions in the answer to your question by saying: ultimately, I felt (sad or scared or angry etc) because… (Say the first reason that comes to mind.) Once you have the emotion(s) and the reason(s), you are ready to put them together to create the Root-Cause Reason for the problem you want to heal:

Root-Cause Reason Statement

$$= \text{Emotion(s)} \quad + \quad \text{Reason(s)}$$
(What you felt) (Why you felt that way)

(Examples include: "Sad, scared and vulnerable Dad left" or "Angry forced to move house" or "Scared Mum so weak", etc. I have shared approximately 300 real-life Root-Cause Reasons in Appendix 2 to help you understand what you are looking for here.)

When you find a Root-Cause Reason, rate it:

> **ASK: On a scale of 0 to 10, with 10 being "very high emotion and feels true", how would I rate (state Root-Cause Reason)?**

Root-Cause Reasons that have the power to justify an unhealthy belief or cause a chronic condition or persistent life problem usually have the emotional intensity of 8, 9 or 10 out of 10 (with 10 being high emotion). If your RCR scores 7 or less then you might want to further explore the reasons why what happened was a problem for you, or see if there is a more emotionally significant Root-Cause Event to work on.

• • •

Quick Timeout to Check In

By this point in the method you should have discovered a Root-Cause Reason; this is a short sentence that summarizes why the Root-Cause Event was a problem for you then. Don't forget:

just because this sentence may feel true, that does not make it absolutely true. All it means is that the younger you, based on the limited life experience you had at the time, felt justified in feeling bad. If you have found an emotionally charged Root-Cause Reason then great! You are only two steps away from making peace with your past. The hard part of the method is over; now I suggest you immediately move on to resolve it.

• • •

Resolve Your Root Cause

PAY CLOSE ATTENTION! This is a very important moment in your life. The purpose of Step 4 of the method is to heal any Root-Cause Reasons that might be justifying the existence of toxic beliefs. Remember: problems are only problems today because of the incorrect conclusions you've come to in the past. And the even better news is your beliefs are easy to change.

You are now going to come to a new, healthier conclusion about the Root-Cause Event and, in the process, let go of any emotions associated with the Root-Cause Reason(s). The end goal of this step of the method is to be able to think about the past event and Root-Cause Reason and feel totally neutral.

To be able to feel at peace when thinking about events that used to cause you negative emotions is evidence that any toxic belief(s) stemming from the event have been healed. You quite literally no longer believe it is justified to feel bad about what happened. You've evolved beyond it being a problem for you.

Give yourself a pat on the back in advance because you are doing great work! Coming to more compassionate conclusions about past events can allow balance to be naturally restored in your body because the reason(s) for the imbalance have been removed. It can also help your external life improve, due to the body–life bond.

The Hard Part Is Over

Becoming aware of your Root-Cause Reasons is the hardest part of the process. From now on, your healing journey gets easier. It is the job of your infinitely powerful inner intelligence to take care of the details. Your job is to let yourself be at peace with your past – which is easier and less stressful than resisting what happened – so that your mind can give your body the green light for healing to take place.

Remember, the mind–body connection means that changing your mind causes changes to occur within the body. You may even find that your "inner pharmacy" immediately gets to work healing any physical conditions the moment the new messages start being sent between your mind and body. Sound good? Great, now keep up the brilliant work you've started by moving on to…

STEP NO. 4 **Why Not A Problem Now?**

(New Conclusions with New Information) Hold the Root-Cause Event in your mind as you answer the following question:

> **What can I know now that, if I had known it in the past, I would have never felt (state Root-Cause Reason) in the first place?**

You may need to ask yourself this question a few times to explore several positive and loving learnings. You are looking to find alternative ways of perceiving the past event that would make it impossible to maintain the Root-Cause Reason you've already found. (By this, I'm not saying your goal is to be happy that the bad thing happened; neutral will be enough for the healing to happen.) You will know you've found it because you will feel a sense of relief.

Other questions you can ask to explore positive and loving ways of thinking about past events include:

- What do I need to know or learn, the knowing or learning of which will allow me to be at peace with what happened?

- For this to have been a problem then, what did I need to not know? Or, for this to be a problem then, what was I pretending not to know?

- If a friend had this problem, what advice would I give them to help them be more at peace with what happened?

- Is it possible for me to be at peace when I think about this event at some point in my life? (The answer to this question is always "Yes, it's possible" – even if you don't know how, yet!). Once you've got an inner "yes", ask: Okay, what could I know at that point in the future so that I could feel at peace then?

- For me to be at peace with this memory, once and for all, what do I need to say now?

The moment you find a positive and loving learning that makes peace with the original event and disproves the toxic belief, move on to Install the Knowing:

TOP TOOL   **Install the Knowing**

Timing is everything when installing the knowing. It must be done immediately you discover the learning you need.

It works because any justifications you had in feeling bad about the Root-Cause Event are undermined and stop feeling "true" and you no longer have any justifiable reason to continue feeling bad. You are quite literally taking the new-found positive and loving learning and installing it in your body–mind. It is powerful and, when used correctly, can be very quick and highly effective at completely clearing all negative emotions linked with the Root-Cause Event and Root-Cause Reason, and immediately heal the toxic belief.

STEPS TO INSTALL THE KNOWING

Get positive and loving learning using Step 4, then:

STEP NO. 1 **ASK: Where do I know this in my body?**

(Notice where within your own heart, chest, solar plexus and stomach this knowing is.)

STEP NO. 2 **ASK: If the knowing had a colour, what colour would it be?**

(Any colour is fine, so trust your first answer.)

STEP NO. 3 **Keep that knowing there and close your eyes.**

Then use your imagination to go to the past, with that knowing, and play the movie of the old memory from beginning to end, but this time with the new positive and loving learning. For example: *I have the red knowing in my heart that I am loved.* Play the memory from start to finish a couple of times.

STEP NO. 4 **Come back to now by opening your eyes.**

This exercise should take up to 30 seconds. If the Root-Cause Event is traumatic and you don't want to imagine it happening again, then once you're clear about where in your body the knowing is, progress to using the Emotional Freedom Technique (EFT) to clear the emotions and install the positive learning. See Chapter 7 for full instructions.

Immediately after you have installed the knowing, open your eyes and take your attention away from the problem and memory for a moment by distracting yourself. Look at a picture on the wall, notice something you can hear nearby or sing a few seconds of a song that lifts your spirits. Do whatever it takes to temporarily take your attention away from what you've been working on. Then, once you've done that, you are ready to move on to the final step of the method…

STEP NO. 5 **Test the Work**

(Explore How Emotionally Neutral You Feel) Testing the work is as important as every other step of the Mind Detox Method. Most people have a convincer of three. By this I mean they need to test the work three different ways for the mind to be convinced that the change has happened. It is vitally important that your mind feels convinced because this helps to activate the healing process. It also helps the mind to begin proving the new healthier belief right. You will find that, during and after you test the work, your mind will start finding evidence to prove the new belief correct.

Enjoy this natural process and use it to your advantage by consistently acknowledging that the change has happened and that it is now safer and easier for your body to heal. Here's how you test the work:

> TEST THE ROOT-CAUSE REASON: On a scale of 10–0, with 0 being "the emotion is completely gone now and I feel neutral", how would I rate the old Root-Cause Reason? (You may want to say the Root-Cause Reason out loud and notice how neutral you feel now.)

> TEST THE PAST: On a scale of 10–0, with 0 being "the emotion is completely gone now and I feel neutral", how would I rate the Root-Cause Event? (You might find that the memory is still there, but the old emotion is gone and you now feel more neutral.)

> TEST THE FUTURE: Think of a time in the future when "something like this might happen, but this time, notice how differently I respond". Okay?

If the answers to the above questions are all 0/10 and you feel neutral, then great. Well done for all the great work you've done and congratulations!

. . .

Getting Your Score to an Absolute Zero

Mind Detox is entirely focused on resolving the mind-based root causes of problems, rather than treating the surface-level symptoms.

Negative emotions are caused by toxic beliefs because they are what determine whether you allow or resist. Negative emotions are always only symptoms of justified resistance, never the cause.

No Toxic Belief = No Resistance = No Negative Emotion

Make sure when you're doing this work that you do not fall into the common trap of focusing all of your energy on trying to get rid of the negative emotions. They will go naturally when feeling bad is no longer justified.

I invite you to treat the surface-level symptoms of negative emotions as signals that there must be residual resistance. We only use the emotions as a useful gauge to determine whether or not you've come to new conclusions yet and healed the toxic belief. So having installed the learning into your Root-Cause Event, if the scores from the questions Test the Root-Cause Reason or Test the Past are *above* 0 check the following:

CHECK NO.1 Antidote Learning

Consider this: *Does the learning I've installed un-justify the negative emotion?* By this I mean: is it the antidote learning to the reason you feel bad? For instance, if you were "scared of dying", have you installed "I survived"? If you have not installed an antidote learning yet, then consider what learning you need to know now that would completely undermine and un-justify the Root-Cause Reason, then install it.

CHECK NO. 2 Root-Cause Reason

If you still feel a negative emotion, but have installed the antidote learning, then it often means you've resolved the Root-Cause Reason you've already found, but there may be more stemming from the same Root-Cause Event.

In other words: Are there more Root-Cause Reasons associated with the Root-Cause Event? Have you worked on the anger you felt, but not addressed the fact that you also felt sad or scared? Consider this: *What else about what happened was a problem for me?* Use the questions in Step 3 to explore other Root-Cause Reasons and resolve them using the method.

CHECK NO. 3 Root-Cause Event

Sometimes, multiple events can combine to create a toxic belief. In cases like this, there might be another event, perhaps earlier or more recent, that you need to work on now. Consider this: *What other event in my life is the cause of the problem?* Trust your mind to give you other event(s) that need working on so that you can be at peace with the past and heal any beliefs that might be negatively impacting your body and life today.

All In One Place

I am aware that I have taught the method alongside a commentary of each step, so you are clear on what you are aiming to do at each part. Once you know the method, I recommend you use the at-a-glance summary of the 5-Step Mind Detox Method in Appendix 1 (page 199) for quick reference and ease of use. I've also provided a D.I.Y. Mind Detox Tool in Appendix 1 (page 202) for you to use.

Still Feeling Something? Don't Fret!

If you *still* feel any negative emotions relating to the Root-Cause Event or Root-Cause Reason, it means that there is a part of your mind that still feels justified in feeling bad. This is a blind spot. I recommend you re-read Chapter 4 to deepen your understanding of the ten ways of re-remembering the past in a more positive light. Alternatively, you can continue on to Chapter 7 and use the Tapping Technique on your Root-Cause Reason, as this can help detox the more stubborn emotions that are lingering within your body–mind.

More Tools To Heal For Real

Whenever I'm faced with more tricky Root-Cause Events and Root-Cause Reasons I will use other tools that I've learned along the way, including:

- Emotional Freedom Technique (EFT)
- My Conclusions
- Decision Destroyer
- Parts Integration
- Getting Your Goals Process
- Pink Light Technique

To discover the power of these additional healing techniques, which can be used alongside the Mind Detox, turn to the next two chapters now.

CHAPTER SEVEN

The Tapping Technique

• • • • • •

HOW TO USE THE EMOTIONAL FREEDOM TECHNIQUE IN A MORE POWERFUL WAY

I CANNOT BREATHE. *My emotions about the past event are so intense I can't bring myself to even attempt Mind Detox.* These are the words of a woman called Karen, who was attending one of my retreats in Turkey. I remember sitting with Karen as she started sobbing. At that moment, we were sat on one of the big loungers in the juice bar of the venue, which looked out over the turquoise-blue water of the nearby pool. Surrounding the pool were tropical trees swaying in unison, as the cooling afternoon breeze played within the palms. There was also a child playing with her mother in the pool and the sweet song of the child's laughter; perfecting the stunning scene happening all around us.

Karen was suffering so much because she had left the safe place of the present moment and got completely caught up in the unhappy story from her past event, which was occurring in her mind. I invited her to engage GAAWO to return to the reality of now (which, as I've described, was very pleasant), but on that occasion she couldn't bring herself to do it. The memory was so significant for her, it was stealing all of her attention. And as she continued to dwell upon the memory, she continued to miss the peaceful presence of the present moment and felt only her negative thinking instead.

On rare occasions like these, when memories trigger intense emotions that make it hard to focus on the task in hand, then alongside Mind Detox I will use the Emotional Freedom (Tapping) Technique. I find it to be a great way to take the edge off things and allow for more clarity, comfort and calm. The physical movement and activity can help people to get out of any potential horrors occurring in their head and, instead, back into the safe place of the here and now.

So that day, sitting with Karen in the juice bar, I invited her to start tapping on a specific part of her hand, as she repeated the Set-Up Statement from the Tapping Technique. I then guided her through the series of 14 other points to tap on around her body, and as we did, she eased her way back into *now*. From this more resourceful state of mind, and with less emotion distracting her from doing Mind Detox, we were able to complete a successful mentoring session.

• • •

The Tapping Technique

Often described as physiological acupuncture, the Emotional Freedom Technique (EFT) is a simple yet highly effective method for calming and clearing intense emotions. It involves tapping on certain "meridian" points around the body, which correspond with acupuncture points, while saying statements relating to the problem that you wish to release and resolve.

EFT has proven successful in thousands of clinical cases, and I have used it many times to help people to comfortably and quickly let go of all types of negative emotions, heal toxic beliefs and even cure health conditions. I've also shown its effectiveness during a couple of my television series, which demonstrated the power of *tapping* alongside Mind Detox.

As mentioned in Karen's story at the beginning of this chapter, I usually use EFT if someone drops into intense emotions that are making it hard for them to continue with the Mind Detox session. (Please see the Top Tips on page 144 if this ever happens to you.) In moments like these the person is so caught up in their emotions that they are not able to listen to me, let alone answer my questions. I also turn to EFT if I get the sense someone is highly kinaesthetic and would benefit from incorporating a more body-based intervention into their self-healing strategy.

TOP TIP **If You Hit a Wall of Intense Emotions**

If when using Mind Detox you uncover a memory that has intense energy associated with it, I then immediately take a few simple steps to shift your emotional state before continuing.

Due to the mind–body connection, you are physically wired to feel certain ways when doing certain things with your physiology. Putting your shoulders back, puffing your chest up and out, taking a few deep breaths, looking up at the sky and putting a big smile on your face (even if at first it feels fake) can all help to quickly create a better state of mind.

It is also advantageous to engage the GAAWO technique (taught on page 107) to the best of your ability. This will calm your mind and help you to stop feeling whatever you are thinking about so intensely. When doing so, remember the three golden rules that I outlined previously (on page 107), because GAAWO will only work if you actively engage it and keep it engaged without stopping to check if the emotions have gone.

Engage GAAWO and allow all the emotions some space and time to subside.

There is no need to ever suffer when doing Mind Detox. Remain in charge of your mental and emotional states and proceed with my method once you feel ready. Finally, there is always help at hand: visit my website to organize mentoring with me and I will gladly support you in achieving peace with more challenging past events.

Tapping On the Right Thing

One of the most common comments I hear from people using EFT is that they are not sure if they are "tapping on the right thing". This is because the technique involves saying or thinking certain statements as you tap on the different body parts.

Most people only know to refer to the problem they are dealing with or the main emotion they are feeling, which are rarely the right things to tap on. Another problem many people encounter when using EFT is that they feel temporary relief from tapping the negative emotion(s) away, but find the emotions return over time. In my experience, combining EFT with Mind Detox solves both of these common concerns.

Don't forget, focusing solely on getting rid of undesirable emotions is still treating the symptoms of your problem, not the cause. To resolve a problem once and for all, it is vital that you clear the belief-based justifications for feeling bad that exist in your mind. It is your toxic beliefs that cause you to resist life and *then* experience negative emotions as a result.

As long as you believe it is justified to feel negatively when certain circumstances occur, then the problem will appear to "come back" in the future. The reality is that, if you only *tapped away* your emotions without healing the belief(s) causing them, it was never "fully gone" in the first place.

Instead of tapping on anything and everything, Mind Detox enables you to use EFT in a precise way. I've repeatedly found it to be incredibly effective to tap on the Root-Cause Reason statements, which you are able to discover using my method. This releases the mind-based justifications for feeling bad and helps you to make peace with your past and enjoy long-term health and lifestyle benefits.

Using EFT With Mind Detox

Begin by clarifying the Root-Cause Reason (using Steps 1–3 of the Mind Detox Method), and then follow these steps:

STEP NO.1 The Set-Up Statement

While tapping the Karate Chop (KC) point located on the side of the hand (see Diagram 1), repeat the Set-Up Statement three times:

> *Even though I (*state Root-Cause Reason*), I love and accept myself.* For example: *Even though I'm sad my dad left, I love and accept myself.*

STEP NO.2 The Round of Tapping

Tap seven to nine times on each of the meridian points while repeating the Root-Cause Reason at each point (see Diagram 1 on the next page for location of meridian points).

At-A-Glance List of Meridian Points		
1 – TH: top of head	6 – CH: chin	11 – IF: index finger
2 – EB: eyebrow	7 – CB: collarbone	12 – MF: middle finger
3 – SE: side of eye	8 – AP: armpit	13 – LF: little finger
4 – UE: under eye	9 – L: liver	14 – KC: karate chop
5 – UN: under nose	10 – TH: thumb	

STEP NO.3 Repeat Round with Positive Learning

Tap seven to nine times on each of the meridian points (TH to KC) again, but this time feel free to say positive learning (see Chapter 4 for suggestions) on some of the points – this can help you to "tap in" healthier ways of perceiving yourself, others and life.

Diagram 1: EFT Points

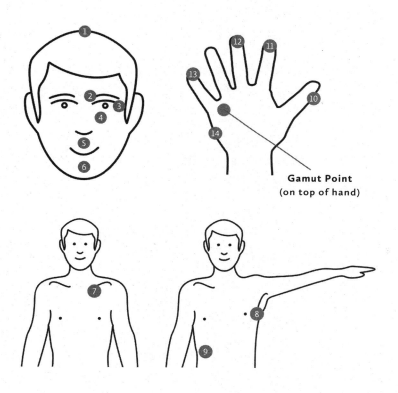

Gamut Point
(on top of hand)

STEP NO. 4 **Re-Rate Emotional Intensity**

Take a deep breath and measure the problem again, using the
Step 5 questions from my method:

> **TEST THE ROOT-CAUSE REASON: On a scale of 10–0,**
> with 0 being "The emotion is completely gone now and I
> feel neutral", how would I rate the old Root-Cause Reason?

> **TEST THE PAST: On a scale of 10–0, with 0 being "the**
> emotion is completely gone now and I feel neutral", how
> would I rate the Root-Cause Event?

TEST THE FUTURE: Think of a time in the future when something similar could happen, but this time, notice how differently I respond. Okay?

If your score is higher than 0, repeat the sequence from 1–4 with the new Set-Up Statement:

> *Even though I still feel "sad Dad left" I deeply and completely love and accept, appreciate and respect, honour and forgive myself.* Then on each point, say, for example, *Remaining "sadness about Dad leaving".*

Remember: if after doing EFT the emotion stays above 0 it means you have a blind spot justifying the emotion; in this case explore Chapter 4 and install the learning you need so you no longer feel justified in feeling any negative emotions associated with the RCE or RCR. Alternatively, turn to Chapter 8, where you will find additional techniques for healing.

TOP TIP In Case of Emotional Emergency

When up against an overwhelming emotional memory that means you are finding it hard to continue with the Mind Detox, on these rare occasions, do not attempt to work out what the real Root-Cause Reason might be just yet. I recommend using a simplified Set-Up Statement by thinking or saying out loud the words: "Even though I feel these emotions, I love and accept myself." Then, as you do the round of tapping, simply think or say the words "This emotion" – as you tap on each point. Do one or two full EFT rounds and then return to do the full 5-Step Mind Detox Method. At this point you can use EFT too, if you want.

CHAPTER EIGHT

The Master Manifestor

. . . . . .

TOP TOOLS FOR CREATING MORE SUCCESS

I CANNOT CREATE. *I self-sabotage my own success.* I had been working in the field of coaching and therapy for a few years and noticed that I had hit a wall when it came to "getting out there", marketing myself and sharing my true talents with the world. Opportunities would present themselves but I had a tendency to self-sabotage. I would delay (or even forget) getting back to people or not convey the knowledge and skills that I *actually* had. I was often talking myself down (believing I was just being humble), but the truth was I was very uncomfortable being honest with others about "who I am" and my capabilities. If I were ever complimented I would have instantaneous amnesia about the positive feedback. But if I received what I felt was criticism, it would hurt to my core and I'd dwell on it for days. I turned to Mind Detox to understand why and resolve the possible cause of my actions.

"What event in my life is the cause of my self-sabotaging that, when resolved, will cause the problem to disappear? If I were to know, what age was I?" The memory that came was sitting in form class at school, around age 13. I could even remember the exact location of where I was in the room and who was sitting nearby.

Out of the blue, one of the more "cool kids" announced to everyone, "Sandy is gay." Within a day or two the rumour had spread like wildfire through the population of the entire school. From that moment on, I was bullied for being a "poof". I became ostracized and outcast, leading to much loneliness and hurt, from the constant name-calling and bullying.

"What was it about what happened that was a problem for me?" It made me feel *"Hurt, isolated, rejected and bullied because one person said something bad about me."* (Incidentally, before continuing let me be clear. Of course it is not *bad* to be gay. But it was bad for me, then, because it wasn't true and was said with the intention of hurting, bullying and ultimately ostracizing me.)

Immediately I could see the link between this unresolved past event and my unconscious reluctance towards getting publicity in my present-day business life. Back then, *one person* had said something *bad* about me and everyone believed it. Not only that, but it had hurt, badly, due to the subsequent rejection and bullying that occurred. I would naturally prefer to avoid being hurt in the future, so my unconscious mind was protecting me from future hurt by limiting my public exposure.

I turned my attention to resolving the root cause. "What can I know now that, if I had known then, would have meant I would have never felt hurt, isolated, rejected and bullied in the first place?" I now know that it is not a bad thing to be gay. I am also not gay, but even if I were, it would be perfectly fine by me. I successfully survived every event of bullying and despite disliking the past moments, life had moved on and there are many occasions in my life when I've been fully welcomed and loved by others. Although it felt like "everyone" had rejected me, there were still people around who accepted me. I *did* have friends at school, and even though they occasionally also bullied me, they did it to fit in, too, and later in life they told me they'd always liked me. Every kid who bullied me was doing their best to fit in and feel safe at school. I am also much more capable of spending time alone than I thought then, and enjoy my solitude today. After installing these new-found "knowings", all associated memories linked to being bullied at school (of which there were many) felt emotionally neutral, along with the root-cause reason.

Within a matter of months of doing this Mind Detox, I was invited to take part in my first television series, which was aired on several channels in 30+ countries around the world.

• • •

The Belief–Life Connection

Despite Mind Detox being a tool for getting peace with the past, doing so can actually empower us to create a fantastic future. We explored the belief–body bond in Chapter 2. Now let's turn our attention to how our beliefs impact our external life, too.

Although you may consciously think about the kind of life you want, it is actually your unconscious mind that is going to help you to get it. Here's how it works: Your unconscious mind gathers a huge amount of data about your external environment, but only passes a small percentage of the information up to your conscious awareness, thus making your conscious experience of life a vastly edited version of reality.

To help you understand the implications of this internal filtering process I invite you to imagine that you are outside and it's raining heavily. Every second about 400 billion droplets of rain fall from the sky and every second you reach out and catch just a handful of the raindrops, approximately 2,000 droplets. In this analogy, you are only consciously aware of the raindrops that land on your hand and unaware of the billions of raindrops that are falling all around. The same is true for your version of reality.

To help you avoid being overwhelmed, your unconscious mind only lets you become aware of what it *believes* is important and relevant to you. Your beliefs are a key determinant of what things "land on your hand" i.e. those that you are aware of, and what things "fall to the ground" without you being consciously aware of them ever existing. In short, what you believe, you will see.

> *Your conscious mind is the goal-setter whereas*
> *your unconscious mind is the goal-getter.*

The implications of this are huge when it comes to goal-setting and creating changes within your external life and world. In essence it means "the outer reflects the inner". The life that you see all around you is in large part a projection of your beliefs, attitudes and expectations. If you believe the world is an unsafe place, then you will filter out safety and find more danger. If you believe that "all men are mean" then you will meet guys who reflect your belief.

This chapter includes additional tools that I've used alongside Mind Detox with great success. They are especially useful for manifesting more external success, so I wanted to make sure you had access to them too, including:

- My Incorrect Conclusions
- Decision Destroyer
- Parts Integration
- Getting Your Goals Process

As a summary, the My Incorrect Conclusions tool is a simple way to clarify any toxic beliefs messing with your manifesting abilities. Decision Destroyer is a way to challenge these beliefs and have them start to lose their power. The Parts Integration exercise helps you to find and integrate any conflicting parts in your mind that could stop you from getting peace with your past and living a more positive life today. And finally, the Getting Your Goals Process clears the mind-based blockages that might prevent you from enjoying the life success you want.

. . .

TOOL NO.1 **My Incorrect Conclusions**

Remember: unhealthy beliefs are incorrect conclusions that you've come to at some point in your past. But when was the last time you sat down and made a list of your beliefs? It's not really something we tend to do too often, despite it being such an important task; they are determining many of our life results, after all. This is an easy exercise for clarifying any conclusions that you've come to along the way, which you may not even have been aware of believing.

INSTRUCTIONS

PART NO.1 **Starter Sentences**

Without editing your thoughts, or overthinking it, finish the following sentences with the first words that come to mind. Aim to get a few answers for each starter sentence.

> *I'm...*
> *I'm not...*
> *I always get...*
> *I always feel...*
> *I'm too...*
> *I will never...*
> *It's hard to...*
> *I'm the sort of person who...*

PART NO.2 **Life Areas**

Now hold the following life areas in your mind and notice the first thoughts you have. For instance, for money, you might have a thought: *It's hard to make money* or *I will never get out of debt*. Or, for love/intimacy, you might think *I will never meet my soulmate*. Notice the first thoughts that come to mind when you think about the following areas and note them in a journal:

- Family/friends
- Love/intimacy
- Career/work
- Money/wealth
- Spirituality/inner peace

Found any toxic beliefs? Use Mind Detox (in Chapter 6) to find out when you came to the conclusion(s) and cleanse them from your mind, for good. But before that, why not give this following exercise a go, as I've found it great for undermining the power of certain beliefs – making your work with Mind Detox even easier.

• • •

TOOL NO.2 Decision Destroyer

Imagine you catch yourself (or a friend) saying an unhealthy belief like, "People I love always leave me" or "It's hard to make money" or "I can't lose weight". There are a couple of questions you can ask to challenge the incorrect conclusion and come to new conclusions that help rather than hinder you.

The interesting thing about beliefs is that there was often a moment prior to forming the belief when you either consciously or unconsciously made a decision. This means that many unhealthy beliefs are preceded by, or based on, an unhealthy decision. This exercise can help you to go back in time (in your mind), make a more positive decision and, as a result of this, start forming healthier beliefs.

INSTRUCTIONS

Temporarily hold the unhelpful belief in your mind and trust your first answer to the question: *When did I decide that?* You may get a number and/or a memory popping into your mind. Amazingly, most people I ask this question of immediately remember the exact moment they formed the unhealthy belief. Once you have a possible memory, ask: *What was I deciding before that?*

Keep asking the second question (going back further and further in time) until you find a decision that is purely positive and loving. It may feel as though you are making it up and that there is no way of genuinely knowing what you were thinking then; this is completely normal. The purpose of this exercise is to track back in your mind until you come across a more positive decision. (Which is probably going to be the opposite of the unhelpful belief!) Then take a deep breath and come back to now, bringing the positive decision with you. Trust your unconscious mind to do this for you. You may now find that, if you think about the old unhealthy belief, it feels less true.

• • •

TOOL NO. 3 Parts Integration

The Parts Integration exercise helps you to find and integrate any conflicting parts within you that may prevent you from getting peace with your past or living a more productive and positive life today.

One of the most common blocks to healing the Root-Cause Event or Root-Cause Reason is what's called a Parts Conflict. These divide us internally and have us pushing in different directions, making it harder for us to heal and achieve what we want. Have you ever said or heard anyone say anything along the following lines:

*"I really want to stop doing X, but a part of me
wants to keep doing it"* or *"I really want to let go of
Y, but I feel a part of me wants to hold on to it."*?

Within the context of Mind Detox, you have a Parts Conflict
if a part of you wants to let go of the problem and a part wants
to hold on. The part that wants to hold on is like a weed: it can
grow with time and the problem can return. If you think a Parts
Conflict might be blocking your healing or ability to create the
success you want, use this Parts Integration tool. It will help
you be fully congruent in your thoughts, feelings and action,
which is absolutely fundamental for being a master manifestor.

INSTRUCTIONS

STEP NO.1 Invite the Negative Part Out

Say: "I would like to invite out on to the palm of one of my
hands the part that wants to hold on to the problem." Then
hold one of your hands out in front of you, palm facing
upwards, as though the part has come out and is sitting on the
palm of your hand.

STEP NO.2 Invite the Positive Part Out

Now invite out the part that wants to let go of the problem.
Say: "I would like to invite out on to the palm of my other
hand the part that wants to let go of the problem." By this
point you should have both of your hands out in front of you,
with one part sitting on one hand and the other part on the
other hand.

STEP NO.3 Find the Highest Intention of the Negative Part

Each of the parts has a positive highest intention. Starting with
the negative part, ask: "For what purpose does this part exist?"
Keep asking: "For what purpose ..." (including your previous
answer in the question) until you find a positive intention for

the negative part. For example: "For what purpose do I hold on to the fear of failure?" Keep asking and you might find that the intention is to "stay safe", so that you "survive", can "keep living", have a "good life" or so you ultimately "feel happy". By this rationale, the highest intention is to be happy.

STEP NO. 4 **Find the Highest Intention of the Positive Part**

Do the same with the positive part until you find the same highest intention. Ask: "For what purpose does this part exist?" Keep asking: "For what purpose ...?" (including your previous answer in the question) until you find a positive intention for the negative part. For example: "For what purpose do I let go of the fear of failure?" Keep asking and you may find the intention is to "go for what you want", so you are "more adventurous", "explore more" and finally so you ultimately "feel happy". By this rationale, the highest intention is to be happy.

STEP NO. 5 **Put the Highest Positive Intention Inside**

Place the integrated highest intention back into the body (in whatever location feels right) and install it with deep breaths.

STEP NO. 6 **Retest the Work**

Retest the work using Step 5 from the Mind Detox Method. You may find that the emotions now feel neutral or even positive.

• • •

TOOL NO. 4 **Achieving Your Goals Process**

Beliefs can either help or hinder you. This tool helps you to, first, rate your current level of belief in your ability to achieve your goal. Then, if you discover you don't fully believe it is possible for you, you should use the Mind Detox Method to heal the unhelpful belief before going on to do a lovely visualization to help install it in your future.

INSTRUCTIONS

STEP NO.1 **Clarify Your Goal**

Clarity is power. What do you want? Do you want to meet a life partner, achieve a specific financial goal, heal a chronic condition, buy a new home? State your goal now.

STEP NO.2 **Rate Your Current Belief Level**

On a scale of 0–10, with 10 being that you believe it is possible to achieve your goal, how would you rate your current level of belief?

If you do not rate it as 10 out of 10, you may have an unhelpful belief that will undermine your ability to achieve your goal. Continue on to Steps 3–5 to detox your unhelpful belief. Or, if you score 10 out of 10 and achieving your goal already feels inevitable, go straight to Step 6.

STEP NO.3 **Clarify Your Unhelpful Belief(s)**

What are the first thoughts that come to mind when you think about achieving your goal? Examples of unhelpful beliefs include: *I'm not lovable*, *It's hard to make money* and *I will never heal*. You are aiming to find possible beliefs that could be preventing you from achieving your goal.

STEP NO.4 **Heal Your Belief(s)**

4.1   What event in your life is the cause of your unhelpful belief, the first event that, when resolved, will cause the belief to disappear? What age were you? Trust your first answer. State your age now.

4.2   When you think of that time, what is the first person, place, event or thing to come to mind? Trust your first answer and let the memory come back to you now.

4.3.1 What is it about what happened that was a problem for you? How did what happened make you feel?

4.3.2 Ultimately, what was it about what happened that was a problem for you? Write down the Root-Cause Reason now in one sentence: – emotion + reason.

4.3.3 On a scale of 0–10, with 10 being "high emotion and feels true", how would you rate your Root-Cause Reason?

4.4.1 What do you know now that, if you had known it in the past, you would never have (state Root-Cause Reason) in the first place?

4.4.2 For this to have not been a problem then, what would you have needed to believe?

Use Install the Knowing exercise now, using the instructions on page 132.

4.5.1 Test RCR: On a scale of 10–0, with 0 being "the emotion is completely gone now and I feel neutral", how do I rate the old Root-Cause Reason?

4.5.2 Test the past: On a scale of 10–0, with 0 being "the emotion is completely gone now and I feel neutral", how would I rate the Root-Cause Event?

4.5.3 Test the future: Think of a time in the future when something like this could happen, but this time, notice how differently I respond.

STEP NO. 5 **Install a Goal in Your Future**

This final step takes about one minute and is to be done two to three times every day until the goal is accomplished. By doing so you will send a consistent message to your body-world about what it is you want.

5.1   Imagine what you will see, hear, feel, smell and taste when you have achieved your goal.

5.2   Cup your hands in front of you and imagine gently placing the image of what you want in the palm of your hand.

5.3   For a few moments, appreciate it now, as if you've already attracted it into your life.

5.4   Breathe three deep breaths of life into the image of what you want.

5.5   Now, imagine the image of what you want effortlessly rising and flying into your future to manifest at a time that is most perfect for you.

• • •

Up next, I share more tools; this time for moving into the right "heartspace" for healing your relationships and loving your life.

CHAPTER NINE

The Love Lesson

· · · · · ·

HOW TO LIVE A LIFE THAT YOU LOVE

I CANNOT LOVE. *All my relationships end in tears when people I love leave.* Following a series of failed relationships, I wanted to get to the heart of the familiar feelings and behaviours that kept cropping up and messing with my ability to love. I noticed all of my intimate relationships would unfold in a similar way: Things began great, I was relaxed, funny and confident and I saw the other person as my "perfect match". Then, at some point, either I would realize *I loved them* or they would say they loved me and things would quickly head downhill. I would become jealous and judgemental, clingy and uneasy, and find countless convincing reasons for why they were no longer the right fit for me.

We would have drawn-out arguments over stupid stuff. Do you know the kind? Whatever was said, I would come up with a *smart* reason not to accept their reassurances and we'd go around in circles. I wasn't intentionally behaving this way; sucked into my emotions, nothing they said would soothe how I felt and my feelings were doing most of the talking. When the argument finally ran out of steam, I'd often be distant for days. In short, I was difficult to be around until they, quite rightly, left me. I would then be distraught over the loss; regretful for the part I played yet strangely satisfied. My series of failed relationships, and confusing sense of satisfaction when they ended, motivated me to do a Mind Detox.

"What event in my life is the cause of my inability to love, the first event that, when resolved, will cause the problem to disappear. If I were to know, what age was I?" Age 14 came to mind. "When I think of this time, what's the first person, place, event or thing that comes to mind?" I was catapulted, in my mind, back to being on my bicycle, riding towards my best friend's house. I remembered turning in to the street where he lived and stopping outside his house. But before dropping my bike to run up and knock on his door, I noticed something strange. Looking into his front room, I saw all the furniture had vanished. The front room— no, wait, the entire house was empty. He was gone.

"What was it about what happened that was a problem for me?" I felt: *"Sad and abandoned because my best friend left me."* All of a sudden, my relationship failures made so much sense. As long as this root cause remained unresolved, I would be incapable of enjoying any long-term relationship with anyone I loved and/or who loved me. One thing the mind always wants to do is prove itself right. As long as I believed *people I love leave me*, then I would feel the need to push people away until they eventually left. As long as they stayed, something wouldn't feel right, so I would find reasons to explain the way I felt. It also clarified my tendency towards jealousy, as I would always be searching for proof to support my unconscious expectation that they were eventually going to leave me.

"What can I know now that, if I had known it in the past, I would have never felt sad and abandoned because my best friend left me, in the first place?" My best friend was 14 years old and it was highly unlikely that it was *his* choice to pick up and leave. It was safe to assume that it was a decision made by his parents. I also had been away at my family's caravan in the Highlands of Scotland for the entire summer holidays. Back then we didn't have mobile phones, so there was no way he could let me know, even if he had wanted to. Therefore, it wasn't personal and I wasn't abandoned. I also made new friends and have always had great mates in my life.

After healing this memory and Root-Cause Reason, did I go on to marry the next woman I met? No! However, I *did* find the old familiar feelings and behaviours that had ruined my previous relationships didn't happen again and I'm very happy in love today.

...

Let Love Be Thy Medicine

Love, or a perceived lack of it, can be found at the heart of the majority of my own and other people's root causes that I've discovered and resolved using Mind Detox. Irrespective of what the presenting problem is, whether it be a physical condition, an emotional one or a life challenge, the antidote is most often love. Irrespective of how traumatic the past significant emotional event happens to have been, again the antidote is love. And irrespective of the country, culture, age or background of the people from around the globe who I've worked with, love appears to be by far the most powerful force on the planet for bringing about miraculous healings and transformations.

If you are experiencing any kind of chronic condition or persistent life problem, then here is your love prescription:

Do all you possibly can to increase the amount of love you feel towards yourself, other people and your life in general.

Do you enjoy cooking, being out in nature, reading books, drinking coffee with friends? Whatever it is you love doing, do more of it. Consider this as the most fun prescription you've ever received!

If you believe you can't do this, due for example to physical or financial constraints, then you'll need to be creative to work out ways to *still* do what you love, within these constraints. They say, *where there's a will there's a way.* I have confidence in you in finding ways to bring more of what you love into your life. Make it a high priority. Don't view these activities as just "nice" things to do, but consider them as *absolutely necessary* for your self-healing, and commit to doing them. People with a positive purpose tend to prosper, compared to those who lack a love for life. Your purpose each and every day is to love as much as humanly possible.

> *"Love like your life depends on it, because it does."*
> — ANITA MOORJANI

In this chapter I share the Love Lesson, including tips and tools for loving yourself and others, as doing so solves so much. Despite its life-saving impact, the lesson can be summarized in seven words:

You feel love when you give love.

Unlimited Love

I talked earlier about how most of us have been taught to look for love on the outside. In a very innocent way (because they didn't know any better), parents, teachers and peers tend to act in ways that give the impression that love is something you earn and find from the outside, rather than an infinite wellspring existing within.

Due to the conditioning to look externally, it is common to fall into the trap of working hard to *be loved* by having the right kind of body, building a successful career, being surrounded by friends and family and, of course, by finding that special someone. Although all of these things can be lovely, looking to them as your *source of love* can lead to frustration, fear, hurt, sadness, let-downs and loneliness, and cause unnecessary stress and suffering. It did for me.

Many of my relationships ended in tears because of one core misconception in *my* attitude towards relationships, which led to either my partner or me reaching our final straws sooner or later. I believed that relationships were an opportunity to *get* love, when in reality, all relationships offer unlimited opportunities to *give* love. Every. Single. One. We feel love when we give love, but for decades I had the direction of love back to front.

This simple yet significant problem with my perceptions of love and relationships meant I had to perform to be deemed lovable by the outside world and perpetually wait to get love from other people. I believed the amount of love I experienced was down to *them* and, as a result, I didn't feel the love that I yearned for. Not because people didn't love me, but because I was withholding love by waiting to be loved. Consequently, I didn't experience love and frequently felt hurt, played the blame game and defaulted to being the victim of an unloving world. Due to my perceived lack of love, in my more intimate relationships, I spent the majority of my time on the sidelines; questioning whether I was with the right person, weighing up the pros and cons and inevitably finding evidence that perpetuated the problem of a lack of love that I perceived.

Outside-In Love

Turns out I wasn't alone when it came to being confused about the direction that love flows. Rarely when working with people do I find that they come from a place in which their priority is to give love. Usually the focus is on the love that they *didn't get*. With this focus on taking, inevitably we end up with more of an "outside-in love", which puts us on the back foot and makes us more prone to being negatively impacted by what we *receive* from other people and life. With this focus on outside-in love, it appears that someone or something else is in charge of how we feel. If we get the response we want then we are temporarily satisfied and soothed. However, if we don't get it, then we can quickly end up hurt, sad, angry etc. Pointing the finger becomes commonplace as we believe that *our* lack of love (or current negative emotion) is caused by whatever someone else said or didn't say, or what they did or didn't do.

> *As long as we wait to give love after we get love,*
> *we are on the fast track to failure and frustration.*

"I feel hurt, angry, unsafe, unloved... because of a parent, partner, peer ..." These days even the politicians get a mention. And although we feel justified in believing these external people are the source of our stress, suffering, upset or lack of love, if we continue to engage life with an outside-in approach, we will stay powerless victims of the whims of others and our love will remain limited.

As long as you believe other people are causing *your* anger, sadness, fear etc. you will spend your days dealing with the same conflicts, just with different people, or jump from one relationship to the next in the hope that you will finally find someone who is your perfect fit. But if we are honest, with this flawed strategy all we are really doing is searching for people who won't press our buttons, challenge our toxic beliefs or help us learn how to step up and wake up into the embodiment of more unconditionally loving human beings. Personally I want to let go of anything limiting my ability to love unlimited. If you, too, want to move from conflict to connection and find true contentment in love and life, it's time to transcend this fatally flawed "outside-in" attitude towards love.

"It is easier to protect your feet with slippers than carpet the whole earth."

— ANTHONY DE MELLO

Inside-Out Love

Wise people don't pin their hopes for peace and love on the actions of others. The full quote by Anthony de Mello is: *"If peace is what you want, seek to change yourself. It's easier to protect your feet with slippers than carpet the whole of the earth."* I love this quote because it is a super reminder to be more empowered within relationships by adopting more of an "inside-out love" strategy. Instead of being victim to the actions of others, look for opportunities to give love, where love has been lacking. Seek to see what button within you may have been pushed, then be willing to "heal thyself" so that you can become the most peaceful and loving person you know. You'll be amazed by how much better you feel whenever faced with people who you previously perceived as being problematic.

Love becomes limited if we love others with half an eye on whether they love us back. You want to love with every fibre of your body, mind and being. So much so that there is no part of you left to care if any love comes back. Trust me, if you are ever caring if someone loves you back, then you have fallen back into "outside-in love". We feel love when we are giving love, so if you are *really* giving all of your love – with no eye on whether it's coming back – then there will be no sense of anything missing. We only feel a lack of love when we are withholding love; when we have accidentally started loving in a "what comes around goes around" type way. *"I will only show love to you when you show love to me first."* This does not work and is completely back to front. Withholding love only hurts you and as long as you play that game, the other people are less likely to learn what real love is either.

Play instead with aiming to be the person in the room who's raining love, without care or abandon for where it lands, and see how it blows the limits off the love you feel for yourself, other people and life.

CONSIDER THIS: It's obviously nice to hear the words "I Love You" but how does hearing it compare to how *you* feel when you say "I Love You" and mean it? You feel love when you give love. That's the secret. That's the Love Lesson. The people who hurt you or let you down need your love so that they may know what love is. And you need to give them love, for you to find peace within your past and present-day life. It's a genuine win-win. Love is the solution to so many problems. Stop waiting to feel love by getting it from others. Start raining love and notice how it helps your body to heal and your life improve: after all, a successful life is one that is loved by the person living it.

> *"My only regret in life is that I have not said 'I love you' often enough."*
>
> — YOKO ONO

• • •

TOP TIP **When Leaving Is a Loving Act**

Just because you are giving love, it doesn't mean you have to stay within "bad" relationships or stay around people who are unkind. Especially if there is any form of mental, emotional or physical abuse going on. On these occasions, it's time to call it a day and walk away. It's not your job to fix the other person or make them stop their destructive relationship patterns. It is their responsibility to resolve their toxic beliefs, attitudes and behaviours. If this sounds harsh, it is quite the opposite. Walking away can be the very wake-up call they need to heal the stuff that's preventing them from experiencing real love in this lifetime. If you stay, you can actually keep them from the lessons they need. If you find it hard to leave, then do a Mind Detox on why you feel the need to stay in an abusive or unhappy relationship.

Saying this, as long as there is no abuse going on, you may want to invite your friend or partner to read this book to see if they are willing to play within the arena of "inside-out" love; if they are, then there is hope for a much more loving and fulfilling relationship for the both of you.

• • •

TOOL NO.1 **Pink Light Technique**

If reading this chapter you have recognized that you've been more of an "outside-in" rather than an "inside-out" lover, then it's time to turn things around, and this tool is a superb way to start. Through the active willingness to send love to everyone in your life, you can practise giving love without needing to get anything in return. The Pink Light Technique is ancient in origin and is used to heal relationships, especially if there is any hurt, anger or even abuse involved. It heals all pain and suffering between the user and the subject. Incredibly, it has never been known to fail, which I believe is partly because it reduces inner resistance towards others. You stop waiting for people to change or behave more lovingly, and step up into the willingness to let go, be the love you want to see in the world and, if required, finally forgive.

Holding grudges hurts the hands that hold them.

I have no interest in holding grudges because it so clearly hurts me. Sometimes I meet people who I just don't jell with. Other times, I've fallen out of harmony due to differences of opinion or a sense of being wronged, which is leading to a resistance or rejection of a person or group of people. In the past I would dwell upon how it was *them* that was the problem and then get caught up in my mind justifying why I'm right to dislike and reject them. These days I aim to use the Pink Light Technique as soon as I notice there is a block within me to love anyone in my life.

As you consistently use this short meditation every day, you can discover something quite magical: you are healing *the part of you that is them*. In other words, as spiritual teachers have always said, "we are all one"; the remarkable reality is that you cannot help but help yourself whenever you are willing to heal your relationship with "others". Even if this doesn't make sense right now, give it a go and see how things improve.

INSTRUCTIONS

The Pink Light Technique involves imagining yourself within a sphere of pink light, radiating from your heart, before one by one covering others in the pink light. For anyone you have a difficult relationship with, feel free to have them stand as far away as required to remain completely comfortable. It will even work if you imagine people standing at the horizon, facing away from you. You can also imagine people who make you feel safe standing all around you as you work on especially challenging individuals. No conversation with the other people is required or recommended, and it takes only a moment to cover each person in pink light.

It is best used as a daily practice, either on its own or at the end of your meditation or yoga practice. You only need to do it once a day and if you would like me to personally guide you through it, visit my website (www.sandynewbigging. com), where you'll find an audio recording on the Free Guided Meditations page.

STEP NO.1 Engage GAAWO (see page 107) while you get yourself in a loving space. Remember a time when you felt loved.

STEP NO. 2 In your mind's eye, picture pink loving light radiating from your heart, encompassing you in a pink sphere.

STEP NO. 3 Stay within your pink light sphere for the rest of the exercise. Remember a most loving memory of yourself (this could be recent or from your childhood) and project this aspect of you outside the pink light sphere. Cover this projection of yourself with the pink loving light, still radiating from your heart.

STEP NO. 4 Then, starting with your immediate family—mother, father, siblings, partner, children—imagine them appearing individually in front of you, outside the pink light sphere. If possible, make it an image of them in a loving memory. In your mind's eye, picture yourself covering each of them with the pink light as if you were icing a cake. Cover them with light and then let them go and move on to the next person. If there is someone who you cannot remember as part of a loving memory, just picture them in front of you. If you cannot do this, visualize bringing them in to stand at a distance and/or facing away from you.

STEP NO. 5 Next, do this with anyone with whom you still have an emotional charge or discomfort.

STEP NO. 6 Allow for anyone else to show up (whether you know them or not and still living or already passed), cover them with the pink loving light and let them go as well.

NOTE: In the beginning, this process should take no more than ten minutes a day, eventually getting down to five minutes. If you can't visualize the pink light, that's fine; what is important is the intent. Once someone is done, assume that they are finished for the day. You will get a sense of when someone is "complete" and no longer requires a treatment. Some people will not show up for a while; others, who you didn't expect to see, will suddenly appear to receive their pink light.

This technique has been highly successful for people who have been raped, molested or abused. Runaway children have been known to reconnect with their family within weeks of starting to use it. Although most people using this technique find it easy to do, some – principally, in my experience, cancer patients – can have difficulty doing Step 3. Be gentle on yourself and enjoy the results.

· · ·

TOOL NO.2 Perfectly Imperfect

Due to the incorrect conclusion that love is attained by acting a certain way, many people can start "performing" to be deemed lovable by others – anyone, even complete strangers. They mould themselves to meet the expectations of others and society, and in the process lose their uniquely lovable self by trying to fit in.

The inner love that you really want is unconditional and therefore non-judgmental. It is not a false love taken from others that is founded upon a list of their fixed criteria. It certainly isn't a love based on you looking a certain way, living up to a specific standard or performing in any particular way. The love you want comes from allowing yourself, others and life to be as you/they/it is, now.

Take a break from judging yourself as good or bad, right or wrong, lovable or unlovable. By first learning to love your own perfect imperfectness, you are more able to give others the same gift. The good news is that there is no tablet of stone somewhere that states how you *should* be. So however you are or your life is right now is perfectly imperfect.

"Every stretch mark or thing you may not like about yourself is a ring on your personal ladder to self-love."
— KYLE GRAY

CONSIDER THIS: Do you have an idea of your ideal life? Is there a gap between how things are now and how you think things should be? If life doesn't match up to your mind-based ideal scenarios then you can end up unnecessarily postponing loving it.

On a piece of paper, draw a line down the middle of the page. On one side of the page write down how you, your body and your life circumstances are today. Then, on the other side of the paper, write down how you think you, your body and your life circumstances *should* be. Then, know this: although you may have an idea of your super self and your ideal life, you are not failing or any less lovable if you don't match up to your mind-based conditions.

Take a moment now to let your body, career, relationships, finances and life be enough exactly as they all are. If they were meant to be any other way then they would be already. They might change in the future, but reconnecting with love now involves you letting this moment be enough. Take a break from things needing to be fixed, changed, different or improved. Just allow what you are and let whatever is happening be as it is now. As you do this, you might notice a sense of relief and relaxation within; along with discovery of an unconditionally loving state of being.

• • •

TOOL NO.3 **Om Love Meditation**

Personally I have learned to love more unconditionally through my daily practice of meditation. Meditating regularly allows you to become less judgemental and more willing to experience reality as it is.

Om Is Where the Heart Is

Om is the vibration of creation. Om is known as being the very first movement from stillness, the first sound that comes from silence and the first something that comes from the nothing. Thoughts, on the other hand, are in essence unmanifested potentiality. They are the seeds of creation. As a result, your thoughts are one of the most powerful tools you have to bring what you want into creation.

To align your attention with Om is to align your attention with the infinite power of creation. It can be very powerful. Whatever thoughts you marry Om up with in your mind you can help bring into creation. So if you want more love, "Om Love" is a powerful thought. By thinking it regularly, you harness the power of Om to help bring more love into your physical experience of life.

For the best results, think "Om Love", with your eyes open, throughout your day. Do not repeat it non-stop as you would a mantra, just think it occasionally whenever you remember to do so. Every time you think it you are watering the seeds of your intentions by aligning your attention with the power of the universe. Below are instructions for closed-eyes meditation:

STEP NO.1 **Be Comfortable**

Sit comfortably on a chair or sofa or even lie on your bed. Support yourself with cushions and wrap yourself in a blanket if there's a chance you could get chilly. Simply, be physically comfortable.

STEP NO.2 **Be Allowing**

Close your eyes while remaining gently alert. From the here and now, let your attention rest forward and wide as you allow whatever is happening within your mind, now. This takes no effort, no straining or trying. Continue by very easily, comfortably and gently observing whether there are any thoughts moving through your mind – as though they were passing clouds in the vast sky. Care less about the content of your mind, and more about watching, allowing and continuing to remain gently alert.

STEP NO.3 Be Loving

Gently think "Om Love", then let the thought go. Do not try to hold it in your mind. Just stay gently alert and watch whatever is happening within your body and mind. After a while you will notice that your mind has become active and that you have started thinking. This is natural and a deeply ingrained habit, so go easy on yourself. When you notice that you've been thinking, gently rethink "Om Love". For the rest of your time meditating, slowly go between being gently alert and occasionally thinking "Om Love". Go back and forth, in a very comfortable way. This enjoyable meditation technique can help you to rediscover that love lives within you.

• • •

Compassion Sets You Free

Compassion is a combination of unconditional love and wisdom. It is the ability and willingness to love others exactly as they are, in the knowledge that every person on the planet is doing the best they can and wants to experience peace of mind and love.

Being compassionate means that, if someone else is having a hard time or being difficult, you don't join them by feeling bad too. Instead, you stay peaceful and loving and show them that it is possible for them to get out of the hole they're in.

Although not feeling bad might sound a bit uncaring at first, in reality, it is the only way to truly help others. If you always agree with the other person that they are broken, or get upset with them, you will only reinforce their justifications for being in the hole – which keeps them feeling bad for even longer. I'm sure you don't want that for them, or yourself.

Imagine a friend calls you, upset because they've split up with yet another partner. They tell you, "All men are bastards, let's go out and get drunk!" Compassion wouldn't necessarily agree with them, because it might not be useful for them to continue believing that. If this person keeps creating similar relationships by attracting similar types of men, it is more useful to help them see why it's happening and what they can do to enjoy more loving relationships.

Much better to compassionately say what you see, rather than blindly agree with your friend, talk about your failed relationships all night over too much wine and end up with a hangover the next day. (And perhaps even the start of yet another doomed relationship!)

But on a more serious note: what if you were abused or attacked? Compassion works in a similar way. Although difficult experiences like these often lead to feelings of hurt, sadness or fear, compassion can set you free from toxic emotions like these.

Rather than getting angry or upset about what someone did, for the sake of your own peace and well-being be willing to view them from a more compassionate perspective. They, like you, want to be happy and know they are loved. Every human, without exception, ultimately wants that; the desire is built in from birth. However, at that time in their lives they didn't know how to love or be happy. To get angry at someone for not knowing how to experience peace, love or happiness makes no sense. To be compassionate does.

Maybe they had difficult upbringings without any positive role models, so they didn't know how to treat you lovingly? Maybe they didn't love themselves fully and so projected judgements on to you? Or perhaps they were so critical of you because they wanted to make sure you had the opportunities they didn't? Who knows? Don't try to figure it out; doing so would only be a mind-read. Instead, play with seeing the problematic person through more compassionate eyes. You will be amazed at how free you can be.

> *"Every trauma is an opportunity to transform.*
> *To be courageous and take a leap of heart."*
> — SONIA CHOQUETTE

CHAPTER TEN

The Freedom Formula

· · · · · ·

WHY STILLNESS IS THE SECRET TO SUCCESS

I CANNOT CALM. *Nothing I do delivers **permanent** inner peace.* Turning points often come when you least expect them. Mine certainly did. Everything was going great. Business was now booming. I was on television around the world. My courses and clinics were full and I was running residential retreats at stunning resorts. I had books out with mainstream publishers, was appearing in newspapers, magazines and on radio too. I had a great girlfriend; we were living in an upmarket part of Edinburgh, driving fancy cars and I had more money than I thought possible. On paper, I was living what many would deem a successful life and I had no reason to not feel perfectly at peace. Then one day I woke up to a really scary realization: despite everything going so well, and even after doing so much inner change work, I lacked lasting inner peace.

It was around that time that a friend recommended I try meditation. I remember politely declining, saying that I couldn't meditate. To which they enquired, "How do you know you can't meditate?" After thinking about it for a few moments, I gave my main reason for why I couldn't meditate: "I cannot stop my mind."

Temporarily happy with my answer, I quickly became confused when my friend joyfully declared, "Ah, well you don't have to stop your mind in order to enjoy peace when meditating." To be honest, her response sounded ridiculous.

Everything I'd read and heard about meditation up until then had all pointed to a "still mind" being the main prerequisite to peace. I knew I didn't have a still mind, so had assumed that was the reason I wasn't peaceful. However, she was suggesting the opposite. Confused yet curious, I knew that all my attempts to change or stop my mind – in order to experience permanent peace – hadn't worked, so I agreed to learn to meditate.

Soon after doing so, I began to experience a surprising amount of serenity. So much so, I went on a 10-week meditation retreat to the Greek island of Patmos to be taught by monks, and then spent a further 14 weeks in the mountains of Mexico, with month-long retreats since. During these times I had the opportunity to meditate all day and night, sometimes up to 18 hours a day, and received great guidance along the way. I also took on a Spiritual Teacher and became a monk myself, but that's a story for another time. As you can imagine, diving into such intensive periods of meditation is transformational, bringing with it inner and outer changes both positive and profound.

After graduating as a meditation teacher and discovering that inner peace was easier than I thought, I wanted everyone to enjoy the benefits of my new-found calmer attitude and relationship with life. It is for this reason I want to end the second edition of this book by sharing what I've found to be the formula for freedom and, with it, ongoing inner peace.

The formula has shaped my new way of working: healing the mind with Mind Detox while also healing our relationship *with* life; by drawing upon ancient wisdom and modern meditations.

These additional elements enable you to massively improve how you relate to your mind, emotions, body and circumstance. It transcends the need of always having to fix, change and improve things before you can enjoy some peace. Most importantly, it can stir us from sleepwalking through life – caught up in the movement of our mind – and wake us up to the reality of *who we really are*.

We can discover our Self to be a surprisingly familiar inner presence of peace, which is always present. By waking up to this *inner kingdom of calm* we no longer need to fear or resist life; we love unlimited and discover that the silent solution to all problems is stillness and peace.

• • •

The Ultimate Root Cause

Most people I meet are having an identity crisis, which I believe is the *ultimate* cause of why they have their problem. Quite simply, they believe they are someone or something they're not. They believe they are the voice in their head and, as a result, rely on what it says too heavily for defining who they are and what they are capable of. They believe they are their past. They believe they are what they are feeling emotionally. They believe they are their body, having identified with it from an early age. Or they believe they are their relationship status, job title, religious affiliation or the long list of other labels that they've found to help define who they are.

Wanting to "know thyself" is part of being born human. It is normal to be on the lookout to find meaning from all of the potential sources listed above. Whether aware of it or not, there's a very high chance that you, too, have been exploring the answer to life's big question: *Who am I?* Without proper guidance or personal investigation, it is extremely easy to fall into the understandable assumption of believing that you are the temporary and transient traits that so many others believe themselves to be, too:

- *I must be the voice in my head because it sounds like me.*
- *I must be my emotion because I feel it inside me so intimately.*

- *I must be my body because it's been with me since I was born.*
- *I must be my job title because that's what I tell people I am.*
- *I must be my relationship status because my Facebook page says so.*
- *I must be my religion because it is what I believe in so strongly.*

The list goes on and on. But none of these things are ultimately you. Yes, they contribute to your personality and what you tend to do with your day, but that does not make them you. Why? They are all temporary; they come and go and change. Therefore attempting to find your Self in these transient labels is a bit like trying to stay still in the ocean without an anchor. It's not going to work and you'll find yourself drifting.

Moving from one belief about yourself to another can be very confusing – not to mention highly stressful – if you attempt to define who you are from the things in your life that constantly change and are largely outside your immediate control.

> *What if you are not who or what you think? Are you willing to explore a new way of perceiving and experiencing your Self?*

Until you know your *real self*, you will define yourself in ways that are proven to prevent inner peace. Your past will be a determining factor in your present-day peace. If you've had a difficult past, you will tend to corrode your current contentment by carrying old memories into the present moment. Your peace will also be privy to whatever is happening in your mind, emotions, body and life today, meaning your peace will be forever fluctuating, and fleeting at best. The chances of you taking things too personally and becoming over-controlling also increases, as you pin your hopes for peace on mostly external eventualities. Inevitably, you will postpone your peace; as you will need to wait until your mind, emotions, body and life are your idea of perfect *before* you believe peace is possible.

As knowing *who you are* sits at the heart of true healing, happiness and life success, let's explore further why you may not be who or what you think, so that you can understand and experience the reality of who you *really* are. To keep your exploration as easy and straightforward as possible, let's set a very simple parameter: Who you really are must be the permanent, ever-present aspect of you, rather than anything temporary that comes and goes over time. Sound fair? With this simple measure in mind, let's explore:

WHY YOU ARE NOT YOUR MIND. How do you know you have a mind? You know you have a mind because you are aware of it. This means, within you now exists a mind and something that is aware of your mind. And although your mind is in a constant state of flux, with thoughts coming and going all of the time, the awareness that is aware of your mind is always present and remains unchanged.

WHY YOU ARE NOT YOUR EMOTIONS. How do you know you have emotions? Again, you know you have emotions because you are aware of them. How many emotions have you felt in the past seven days? If you've experienced more than one, which I guarantee is definitely the case, then it means that emotions are also temporary. Despite emotions coming and going, the awareness within you, which is aware of the emotions, is permanently present.

WHY YOU ARE NOT YOUR BODY. How do you know you have a body? Yes, you guessed it. You are aware of having a body. Your body is also constantly changing, but there is something living within the body that is permanent and unchanging. You only have to look at a photo of you from a few months ago and you will see subtle differences. More obvious evidence of the body changing is the fact that you've had multiple "bodies", including a baby's body, a toddler's body, a teenage body … I'm sure you get the point.

As I was writing this book I accidentally chopped off the top corner edge of a finger when cutting into an avocado (I hear it is a very common injury these days!). When the accident happened I was reminded that *I am not my body*, because despite a part of mine missing, who I really am remained fully intact.

If by now you are curious to know the answer to the big question *Who I am?* then this is great news and vital for discovering the truth of who you are, in reality, rather than the mind-made self that so many people are conditioned to believe themselves to be.

Who Am I? I Am Aware

As I've alluded to above, during literally thousands of hours of meditation, I've explored this big question and come to conclude: I am simply the self that is aware. Everything else is a mind-made creation or life circumstance that comes and goes. But that which is aware does not. So who are you? You are the awareness that is aware of the voice in your head and all the other thoughts and emotions happening daily. You are the awareness that's aware of past memories. The awareness that is aware of your body and all the physical sensations and symptoms that occur. The awareness that's aware of all of your relationships, bank balance, the jobs you do, the houses you inhabit and the hobbies that you happen to love.

Even if you've been unaware of it, your awareness has been fully present your entire life. Awareness is what still exists when you are *not* having thoughts or emotions. It is forever with you despite the people in your life moving on, your job titles changing, your body growing older, your home addresses moving and so on; it is the contextual landscape in which everything else in your life occurs. As a result, the importance of being self-aware i.e. being aware of the aspect of your *Self* that is *aware* cannot be overexaggerated. Being self-aware is vitally important for anyone with a genuine desire for peace, more love in life and freedom from stress.

Who Cares?

Why is it so incredibly important to know who you *really* are by experiencing the awareness within? Firstly, because when you do, you discover that your awareness is still, silent, peaceful and free – always. The awareness has never been hurt, scared, anxious, alone or worried about anything. It's been aware of a mind doing these things, but the awareness itself has been at peace the entire time.

If self-awareness being the key to permanent peace *isn't* a good enough reason for you, then consider these questions:

- What part of you cares about what's happened in your past?

- What part of you has judged and resisted so much of your life?

- What part of you has cared so much about how you are feeling?

- What part of you has felt sad, scared, anxious, confused etc.?

- What part of you has worried and suffered over your health?

- What part of you has been so concerned over paying the bills?

- What part of you has stressed over your levels of success?

The answer to every one of these questions is: the mind, ego or whatever you prefer to call the inner "thinker". It's your mind that cares what's happened in the past and continues to resist it to today. It's your mind that judges and engages the resist persist and creates a whole host of negative emotions as a consequence. It's your mind that cares so much about how you are feeling and keeps you working so hard, spending money and running for your life to keep it continuously happy. It's your mind that gets scared, lonely etc. and it's your mind that has done all of these things for so many years that the likelihood of you ending up with a chronic condition has increased. All these problems have been mind-made.

By being self-aware and knowing your real self, to the point that you know you have a mind, but you are not your mind, you step towards a healthier relationship *with* your mind and a liberated relationship *with* life. Instead of feeling so compelled to engage in everything your mind says or does, you can rest into the awareness within and experience a calming clarity instead.

The best news yet: you already have the very tool you need to be aware and rediscover your real self. Engage GAAWO now by being gently alert with your attention wide open. Without thinking about it or planning to do it later, simply engage GAAWO now. Without moving your eyes around, gaze ahead while letting your attention rest wide and open to the left and right, above and below. Continue with me now to be gently alert with your attention wide open and notice what it is like. Can you notice an inner calm or stillness? Has your mind become quieter, to the point of being completely silent? Are you still thinking about the past or future and are you naturally attentive to the here and now?

GAAWO is a wonderful way to be present and aware. By engaging it you immediately experience what your awareness is like, rather than only feel your thinking. As your awareness is inherently still, silent and peaceful and also beyond all mind-made problems, you can in turn experience freedom from any problem.

Many of our problems are perpetuated because we are forever focusing on them by thinking about them. But when you stop that unhelpful habit, you enjoy the ultimate mind detox – a mind clear of all problems. Imagine that! Actually, don't engage your mind again to imagine it, just keep GAAWO'ing to stay in the here and now, which you now know is a place of peace.

Why Freedom Is So Freeing

Freedom is the willingness to experience anything and the ability to do so without suffering. In other words, the more resistant to experiencing *all* parts of yourself and life, the less free you will be. The more you need to control your mind and emotions so they are only "positive", the less free you will be. The more your body has to be a certain way for you to be okay, the less free you will be. And ultimately, the more you need life to be any *fixed way* for you to be okay, the less free you will be. Meaning, freedom requires us to surrender the need to control and cultivate a willingness to experience every last bit of life.

Whether we like it or not, life is happening on a spectrum of possibilities. Sometimes you get what you want, and sometimes you won't. It's not personal; life doesn't have a vendetta against you. Irrespective of how much personal change work you do, including Mind Detox, life has a way of sometimes presenting a different path to what you may have planned for, or thought you wanted.

Sometimes you will be on time and sometimes late. Sometimes you will be financially flush and other times strapped for cash. Sometimes you will have an abundance of love in your life, and at other times, someone somewhere may decide they don't like you. This isn't me thinking negative; it's me being real about the reality of life. Can you relate to it? Does it provide some relief to know you aren't messing up? The Freedom Formula helps you to align with the realities of life, rather than resist them, so that you no longer need to suffer in the face of inevitability.

What can be done about this problematic predicament of not always getting what you want? One option is to get very busy controlling everything, by fixing, changing and improving every orifice of existence so it aligns with your hopes and dreams. This *happy-ever-after* strategy usually involves time, effort and luck to get everything how you want it, and sometimes it simply isn't possible. This fix it, change it, improve it option also does not lead to freedom due to the high amounts of control involved.

The far freer way is to play with the manifesting tools in Chapter 8, while simultaneously surrendering control. In order to live in this way, aim to find an inner balance between having clear goals and intentions to aim for, taking whatever action is required, while letting go of the outcome and being willing to engage without resistance whatever reality reveals.

This second strategy is the most fun and free option by far. It doesn't require you to postpone feeling good until after you've achieved your goal. It is about being at peace as you walk your path, which is possible because the second option involves being self-aware and the cultivation of a healthier relationship *with* life.

The Freedom Formula

Relating to life in an unhealthy way causes resistance, whereas a healthier relationship with life involves a willingness to welcome reality. The mind becomes busy whenever we perceive problems, so by using Mind Detox to stop perceiving people, events or things as problems, it naturally becomes still. Meeting life *where it's at* allows us to live with heaps more peace and harmony. Instead of getting stuck in the holding pattern of fixing one problem after the next, we "move with the perceived punches" and find we dance with life.

A prerequisite of paramount importance for enjoying a healthier relationship with life is to have a healthy relationship with your own mind. When you know *who you are* you also know you are not your mind. Naturally you don't take everything that the mind says or does so personally or seriously. You make peace a priority and know thinking about problems only perpetuates them and corrodes your calm. It is ultimately a waste of your precious time. You don't feel the need to dwell on the past nearly as much, if at all. You know the past is only a mind-made memory, isn't happening in the safe place of now; and that now is the only time when you can live and love your life.

As it is your mind that has been holding on to its perceived problems about your emotions, body and circumstances, you automatically improve how you interact with all aspects of life, if you have a healthier relationship with your mind. With the ability to be self-aware and use Mind Detox to prevent the resist persist and cultivate a purer perception of reality, you find that you now have the formula for a problem-free and peaceful life:

**Know Your Aware Self + Pure Perception of Reality
= Freedom From Problems + Peace with Life**

I hope is that you see the life-changing impact of this freedom formula. If you use Mind Detox to purify your perceptions, you see the reality of any given external situation, where resolution awaits. If you are *also* self-aware and "know thyself" you experience the inner presence of peace, which is also waiting patiently within you. When combined, the result is freedom from persistent problems and a priceless peace with life.

CALMOLOGY: Liberate Your Relationship With Life

Since creating Mind Detox in 2007, I've gone on to create three further transformational techniques: Mind Calm, Body Calm and Calm Cure – with all four techniques collectively known as Calmology. When combined they enable you to change your mind for the better, while also changing your relationship with reality for a liberated life. As within this chapter I'm sharing theory from all four Calmology techniques, here's some context.

After observing the need in my clients and myself for both Mind Detox and meditation, I trained and graduated as an Ishaya Ascension "meditation" teacher in 2009. In 2012 I created Mind Calm, followed by the Body Calm technique a couple of years later. Mind Calm aims to prove that the secret to success is stillness and helps us to move from stress and serenity by getting "peace with mind". Body Calm gives the body the rest it needs to recover and brings about the holistic harmony required for better health. Both Mind Calm and Body Calm consist of powerful ways to meditate and additional supporting principles and resources.

Most recently, Calm Cure was born out of the need to also offer a systematic way of applying my "peace with life" philosophy to heal the Root-Cause *Conflicts* negatively impacting people's present-day experiences. If you are ever struggling with something then it is common to be told to "accept it", "let it go" or "surrender", yet many find it hard to do so because they've been conditioned to do the exact opposite.

In summary, we've been conditioned to *resist* what we don't think we want and be *attached* to what we believe we need. Therefore, if you have a problem, caused by a Root-Cause Conflict, it means you are stuck in the middle of the *conflict combo* of resistance and attachment. What you are in conflict with you keep creating. Therefore, Calm Cure for calming your unconscious conflicts, so that you can calmly coexist with anything that happens during daily life.

When combined, Mind Detox gives you "peace of mind" by getting peace with your past and cleansing toxic beliefs. Mind Calm gives you "peace with mind" by being self-aware and inwardly still now. Body Calm gives you "peace with body" and cultivates the optimum inner climate to help your body heal and stay healthy.

And finally, Calm Cure provides "peace with your entire life" by clearing conflict while empowering you with both the willingness and ability to peacefully experience *anything* that happens on the spectrum of life possibility. (Please see *Next Steps* on page 220 for how to learn Calmology online via my Calm Clan or train and qualify to share it with others.)

The Freedom Formula shared here is harder to apply in *real life* if you continue to fight your thoughts and feelings. So let's focus on these two key elements now, to ensure that you are clear how "peace with mind" and "peace with emotions" can be achieved.

Peace with Mind

Imagine you are outside on a clear sunny day looking up at the big blue sky. Naturally, you feel calm, relaxed and wonderfully well. Then, out of the blue, a bird flies across your field of vision. Upon noticing the bird, you take your focus away from the still sky to instead track the movement of the bird as it flies on by. But you don't stop there. You then start thinking about the bird – "I wonder where it's coming from and going?"… "Why is it flying solo?"… "Oh no, has it lost its friends?"… and before you know it you are no longer feeling as calm or well as you were. Instead, you are now feeling concern for the bird.

What's the bird and sky got to do with keeping calm and benefiting from "peace with mind"? Inside you, right now, there is a big "sky" of awareness and within this awareness there are "birds" flying around – including thoughts, emotions, physical sensations, life circumstances… even the words you are reading now are things you are aware of and therefore "birds" in your "sky of awareness".

You are not your thoughts. You are the peace-filled awareness that is aware of your thoughts.

To experience "peace with mind" you want to become much more interested in and attentive to the awareness that's aware of your mind. By being aware, you immediately experience your awareness instead of feeling your thinking (which can often be negative). You discover that your awareness is still, silent, peaceful, powerful, unlimited and infinite. It is who you really are (as opposed to who you *think* you are) and by being *self-aware* you have inner peace, even if there are thoughts happening in the mind. "Peace with mind" is possible because your awareness is a peace-filled still silent presence; therefore, *peace* is aware of all thoughts.

Let It Go!

Let me also illustrate the benefits of thinking less and being self-aware more, with an analogy shared by my Spiritual Teacher.

Imagine Sam, you and I are together one day and decide to sit beside a road to count the red cars. We find a nearby bench to sit on and start our car-counting game. A few cars pass, a blue one, a silver one and a black one. We just observe them driving past and let them freely come and go. Then we see a red car and count it – one. A few more cars drive by and again we let them, followed by a red car – two. A few more cars pass, including a red one. You and I count it – three. But for some unknown reason, Sam jumps up and starts running as fast as she can up the street – chasing the car – and with a spectacular leap, manages to grab on to the rear bumper of the red car.

You and I look at each other in bemusement as we watch Sam getting dragged up the road behind the red car. By this point, she has lost a shoe, her new jeans are torn and we think we can even see some blood! But if we thought that was peculiar, what comes next takes it to an entire next level.

Sam shouts back at us, "Guys, this car is hurting me!"

With a desire to help her stop suffering as quickly as possible, we shout back, "Sam, the car isn't hurting you, holding on to it is. Let it go, let it go!"

Clearly the red car isn't hurting Sam, but rather her struggle from holding on to it. To quickly stop all the hurt, stress and suffering she simply needs to let go.

So how does this work in the real world and within the context of "peace with mind"? Your thoughts are never the problem, irrespective of how negative they might be. No thoughts have the inherent power to hurt you or cause you any stress or suffering. What hurts and creates problems is holding on to thoughts through the act of thinking. Thinking is simply unobserved thoughts. By being self-aware you can observe your thoughts coming and going and experience peace the entire time. However, if you stop being self-aware, the habit is to grab on to your thoughts, start to think and feel whatever you are now thinking about. In other words, the combination of a lack of self-awareness plus unconscious thinking is the cause of you getting dragged up the metaphorical street, which in reality involves getting dragged through your mind.

The solution is straightforward. Let go of your red cars. Let go of overthinking by making *being self-aware* more important than engaging thoughts about your perceived problem. If you find it difficult to stop thinking, then use Mind Detox to clear the compulsion to keep thinking about it. The rewards for being self-aware arrive fast, due to the peaceful presence of your real self. Thinking is dead compared to the aliveness of now. Choose life.

TOOL NO. 1 Special Stories

This tool, taught to me by my Spiritual Teacher, can help you to start to see the familiar "red car" thoughts that pass through your mind, which you often unconsciously think about. I call this tool "Special Stories" because they are usually personal stories, which you immediately engage with and start feeling. For example: if you have "money" thoughts, you may start worrying. Or if you have thoughts about your relationship then, again, you can feel compelled to think about it at length and suffer as a result.

I can really relate to this one. Any time I had the thought: *Am I with the right woman?* I would feel the need to think about whether I was. Then one day, I used this tool and the need to keep thinking about it dropped dramatically and next time the familiar thoughts arose, I was able to just see them and let them go. I also once saw a story that made me feel depressed. It was a convincing story about me never being able to be truly happy and any time it passed through my mind I would immediately start feeling low.

One day I caught myself thinking about it and gave it a name. I called it my "Mr Melancholy" story. Any time I noticed the old special story happening, I turned to it and said, *"This is just my Mr Melancholy story"* and like magic, it stopped negatively affecting me. It may sound too simple to work, but if you are self-aware and keep calling your stories out, they can quickly lose their power.

INSTRUCTIONS

- Notice if you are busy thinking about a familiar story. Engage GAAWO to be self-aware. This will immediately help you to let go of the special story as you cannot engage GAAWO and continue to unconsciously think.

- Give the story a name. For example, if you always feel left out or left behind, you might call it your *"Cinderella Story"*. If you feel unconfident or anxious, then you could call it your *"Scared of My Own Shadow Story"*. It is helpful if you keep the name of the story light-hearted and funny to you.

- Once you have a name that summarizes the special story, say out loud or think: "This is just my (insert name) story".

- Then re-engage GAAWO and be willing to let it go.

One common habit of the thinking mind is to take everything very personally and seriously. So one of the best ways to improve your relationship with your mind is to take it more lightly. View the mind as just a bunch of random thoughts. It only has power over you if you're not self-aware and you temporarily forget that you are not your mind; you are the vast sky of awareness that is aware of your mind. The sky doesn't care what flies through it. I invite you to stop caring as much about what passes through your mind, too.

• • •

Peace with Emotions

One of the biggest challenges people face when learning to be self-aware and adopting a healthier relationship with life is applying it to their emotions. There is often a deeply rooted habit that keeps them resisting certain "negative" emotions in attempt to only feel "positive". Also, from my experience, emotions can be a major distraction from maintaining self-awareness, as we constantly check in to the mind to think about how we are feeling. This has been one of my greatest challenges and so I've investigated it in great detail.

Anytime we notice an emotions, the mind will often become active by asking two questions: what am I feeling and why am I feeling this way? If you aren't self-aware, you can get caught up thinking *about* your emotions and try to control them.

Cultivating a healthier and harmonious relationship *with* your emotions is much easier when you know the following principles:

- It's completely natural, normal and necessary to feel a spectrum of emotional energies during daily life.

- What you resist will persist and will cause stress and suffering.

- All emotions are temporary, but the power, peace and presence of your self-awareness is permanently present.

- The awareness that is aware of anxiety, sadness, hurt etc. is not anxious, sad or hurt etc. (Re-read this as many times as it takes to really get the magnitude of this principle.)

- The awareness that is aware of anxiety, sadness, hurt etc. is calm, well and free from all emotions – always.

- Recognizing you have temporary emotions but you are not your emotions helps you to more calmly coexist with them all.

- Peace is not the absence of emotions. Peace is a state of being, which you experience whenever you are self-aware and at peace with how you feel.

- Suppressing emotions lowers energy and your ability to enjoy the best life. The more emotions the better as you need energy to heal, create, evolve and wake up.

- Feel your feelings without getting lost in them by remaining self-aware and being alert to *all* that is happening now.

- Emotional freedom comes from being comfortable feeling comfortable sometimes and uncomfortable sometimes.

Words cannot express the importance of exploring these principles and applying them to your own emotional well-being. To help you do this, play with this tool.

TOOL NO. 2 **Hello Energy**

As this may be a very new way of relating to your emotions and there's a chance you may not already be willing to feel the full emotional spectrum, this tool is a wonderfully simple way to begin your journey towards being comfortable feeling uncomfortable.

INSTRUCTIONS

Are you resisting how you are feeling? Lost in your emotions? Struggling to engage GAAWO by staying self-aware? In moments like these, when you're falling into your feelings, do the following:

1. Ask: *What emotion am I aware of right now?*

2. Ask: *Where do I feel the emotion in my body?*

3. Once you've named and located the emotion, turn your attention towards it and say in your mind or aloud the following: *Hello energy, thank you for passing through. You are welcome to hang out as long as you want.*

4. Breathe nice and deep and easy, allowing the energy to move around your body.

WHY THIS WORKS: The first two steps help you to be the observer of the emotion rather than so caught up in it. The simple statement in Step 3 holds within it the intention to allow rather than resist, which helps you to find "peace with" the fleeting feeling. Lastly, we tend to hold our breath when we don't want to feel something, so breathing properly enables the energy to move around your body and helps you to feel empowered by its intensity.

TOP TIP **Don't Pretend**

For this game to give you "peace with emotions" you need to *genuinely* be willing for the emotion to "hang out as long as it wants". Be careful not to say it, but secretly be saying it so the emotion goes away. If you do that, then you are still resisting it and what you resist will persist. Let the energy be present for as long as it wants. The easiest way to do this is to give more of your attention to the present moment happening all around you – using GAAWO – instead of constantly leaving the now to check if the emotion has gone yet. After all, there is always more happening right now than what you're currently feeling. If you leave it alone you will soon notice it will move on, but it ultimately won't matter, as you will no longer have a problem with it being present within you.

It is safe to assume that if you don't want to feel a certain emotion then you will have tried to make it go away before now.

How has that strategy worked? Has the anxiety stopped? Have the depressed feelings disappeared? Probably not. Remember: what you resist will persist. So give this "peace with emotions" approach a go.

Are You Feeling Love, Actually?

I'd now like to make a rather radical suggestion, which can completely transform and improve your relationship with *all* of your emotions. Is it possible that all emotions are actually *love*, but nobody ever told us and so we've ended up resisting love's ever-present presence within?

CONSIDER THIS: You know what you are feeling, right? We assume so. However, have you ever stopped to consider how you know what you are feeling? We've been taught many different names (or labels) for the "different" emotions we experience. Anger. Fear. Sadness. Guilt. Anxiety. Happiness. Hope. Excitement. The list goes on. But what if they are not 100 percent accurate labels? What if you've only ever felt different fragrances of love, fluctuating in intensity?

> *"We walk around with a cathedral of love inside us."*
>
> — MEGGAN WATTERSON

TOOL NO. 3 One Love

How would you relate to your inner energy if you knew it was love? Would you resist it or rejoice in love's ever-present presence?

INSTRUCTIONS

Engage GAAWO by being gently alert with your attention wide open. Place one hand on your heart and one hand on your belly, breathe deeply and allow whatever emotions you are feeling to be present within you, as if you *already* knew that the energy is the presence of love within.

Let go of any specific emotion names or labels that you've been taught, so that you can experience the truth of what you are *really* feeling now. With GAAWO engaged, void of labels and fully willing to let the energy be present within you, what is it like? Is it possible that during your life you haven't been feeling different (positive or negative) emotions, but rather *only* different frequencies and intensities of the same, one, universal energy, which is love? Be self-aware as you continue to let go of any labels. Breathe and let love stretch its wide-open wings within and around you.

• • •

Who Are You? You Are Love

With Mind Detox you can get peace with anything that's happened in your past and, in turn, have fewer reasons to ever need to leave the magnificent moment, where real life is happening. I hope you use Mind Detox, along with the supporting principles and techniques I've shared, to wake up every day into a simmering affection, and ever-increasing love for life. To bring this book to a close there's one final belief that I want to share with you, which sits at the heart of so many chronic conditions and persistent problems: *I am separate from love.* This one belief is the cause of so many issues because it fuels fear, causes people to resist their life and makes people more prone to living in separation rather than in oneness with source.

What if, in reality, the true home of love has always been your own heart? Is it possible that love has never left you and you are one with the love that you've been seeking elsewhere?

Discovering that you are not separate from love reaps rapid rewards. Rather than having to change so that you can *eventually* feel loved, you can *immediately* connect with an inner presence of love now. Take a moment to consider the big implications of this remarkable possibility. You don't need to fix, change and improve yourself (or others) so that one day you can experience love. Instead, love came built in from birth, and enjoying your birthright can be as simple and immediate as tapping into an inner love that is *already* present.

> *Stop trying to be loved and, instead, discover that you are love.*

Imagine if you knew that love was forever within you and that you went about your days experiencing the presence of love within. How differently would you engage with daily life? Would you worry so much about what people think about you? Would you resist what's happened in your past? Would you fear the future? Would you spend time with people who didn't treat you well? Would you hold grudges about not being loved enough by others? Or would you feel freer to be, do and have what makes your heart happy?

> *Knowing you are one with the inner source of love is the secret to self-healing and living a truly successful life.*

Everything in the universe exists within a constant context of oneness-infused love. By bringing your attention back to the present moment by being self-aware, you can discover and experience a permanent inner presence. With practice and persistence, it becomes obvious that the presence you are experiencing *is* love: unbounded, undiluted, unconditional love. When resting fully aware of this inner presence, you are *living in love* and things that you used to see as problems become invitations for you to let go, be free and love being alive.

"Of course there is no formula for life except perhaps an unconditional acceptance of life and what it brings."

ARTHUR RUBINSTEIN

The 5-Step Method

· · · · · ·

AT A GLANCE

Key to Important Terms

ROOT-CAUSE EVENT
The significant emotional event in your past.

ROOT-CAUSE CONCLUSION
The conclusion you came to as a result of the Root-Cause Event happening.

ROOT-CAUSE REASON
The reason why the Root-Cause Event was a problem for you. It is a short sentence with an emotional element and the main reason(s) why you felt the way you did.

TOXIC BELIEF
This is the same as the Root-Cause Conclusion. I use the word "belief" because readers are more familiar with the term. You will discover that all toxic beliefs stem from corresponding Root-Cause Reason(s).

THE 5-STEP METHOD AT A GLANCE

PART ONE DISCOVER the Root Cause

1 **Find Root-Cause Event** *(WHEN did it start?)*
ASK: What event in my life is the cause of the problem, the first event that, when resolved, will cause the problem to disappear? If I were to know, what age was I?

2 **Clarify the Context** *(WHAT happened?)*
ASK: When I think of that time, what's the first person, place, event or thing to come to mind?
Digging-deeper questions: Who was there? Where was I? What was happening?

3 **Discover the Root-Cause Reason** *(WHY was it a problem?)*

3.1 FOR EMOTION – ASK: What is it about what happened that was a problem for me? How did it make me feel?

3.2 FOR REASON – ASK: Ultimately, what was it about what happened that caused me to feel that way?

3.3 RATE ROOT-CAUSE REASON – ASK: On a scale of 0–10, with 10 being "very high and feels true", how would I rate (state Root-Cause Reason)?

PART TWO RESOLVE the Root Cause

4 **Come to New Conclusions with New Info** *(WHY IS IT NOT a problem now?)*

4.1 LEARN FROM THE PAST – ASK: What can I know now that, if I had known it in the past, I would have never felt (state Root-Cause Reason) in the first place?

4.2 LEARN FROM THE FUTURE – ASK: Is it possible that I can be at peace when I think about this old event at some point in my life? If yes, when? Okay, what will I know at that point in the future that will enable me to feel at peace then?

4.3   LEARN FROM THE BLIND SPOT – ASK: For this to have been a problem, what did I need to not know? Digging-deeper question: For it to be a problem then, what did I need to believe? (Helps <u>find</u> a conclusion)

Use the Install the Knowing exercise when you discover a positive and loving learning that makes it impossible for you to have negative emotions associated with the RCE or RCR.

PART THREE   **TEST the Work**

5   **Test that the Root Cause is Resolved**
(Acknowledge Emotional Domino Benefits)

5.1   TEST THE RCR: On a scale of 10–0, with 0 being "the emotion is completely gone now and I feel neutral", how do I rate the old Root-Cause Reason?

5.2   TEST THE PAST: On a scale of 10–0, with 0 being "the emotion is completely gone now and I feel neutral", how would I rate the Root-Cause Event?

5.3   TEST THE FUTURE: Think of a time in the future when something like this could happen, but this time, notice how differently I respond?

D.I.Y. MIND DETOX

WHEN Find Age	What event in my life is the cause of the problem, the first event that when resolved, will cause my problem to disappear? If I were to know, what age was I?
WHAT Root Cause	When I think of that time, what's the first person, place, event or thing that comes to mind?
WHY Root-Cause Reason	How did what happened make me feel? Ultimately, what was it about what happened that caused me to feel that way?
WHY NOT Loving Learning	What can I know now, that if I had known it in the past, I would have never felt any negative emotions in the first place?
Now use the Install the Knowing exercise (see page 132)	

The Top 20 Toxic Beliefs

· · · · · ·

(WITH ASSOCIATED ROOT-CAUSE REASONS)

IRRESPECTIVE of what the physical, emotional or life problem is, during literally hundreds of Mind Detox consultations I've observed the same beliefs appearing time and time again. The top 20 most common toxic beliefs are shared over the following pages. Making sure you don't believe any of them can help you to heal current problems and prevent the onset of future ones.

The Claim

How can I make the claim that these beliefs have the potential to cause physical conditions? Here's how:

1. When I met clients at my clinics, workshops or residential retreats they had a physical condition;

2. After the consultation(s) many clients reported their physical conditions getting better;

3. The only thing we did during the consultation(s) was to help them make peace with their past by discovering and resolving beliefs and associated Root-Cause Reasons.

How to Use the List

Toxic beliefs have Root-Cause Reasons (RCR) that provide mental and emotional evidence that justifies them being true (for you). If you find an unhealthy belief in the Top 20 list that feels true, you then want to find the corresponding RCR(s) that are justifying the belief.

Follow These Steps:

1. Read the list of beliefs and notice whether any of them feel true to you and/or if you have evidence that proves their validity.

2. Once you discover a belief that resonates with you, turn to the subsequent pages to find real-life examples of Root-Cause Reasons (RCR) that, in my experience, I've found to be justifying the toxic belief.

3. Read through the list to find the RCR that most resonates with you. Place a tick in the box beside it. You may notice while reading through that an RCR of your own comes to mind that better fits your personal experience. Write it down if it does.

4. Once you've discovered the toxic belief and corresponding RCR, do your best to remember a problematic event from the past that is linked with the RCR. For instance, if your RCR is "sad I'm bad", then think of a memory in the past when you felt sad because you thought you'd been bad. Having a memory is useful when it comes to healing the belief.

5. Once you have the belief, RCR and memory, go to Chapter 6 and use Mind Detox (picking up the method at Step 4) to achieve peace with your past and, in turn, cleanse the toxic belief.

Reality Is What Is Real Right Now

Don't forget, all you are exploring and changing here is your imagination. You are not time-travelling, and your past is no longer happening. Right now you are safe, and you will remain so throughout. These toxic beliefs may feel true, but they are not absolutely true.

Remembering this can help make the entire process be comfortable – and even enjoyable! If you are in any doubt about your ability to go through this process on your own, contact me for a Mind Detox mentoring session at:

www.sandynewbigging.com

TOP 20 TOXIC BELIEFS

1. "My parents didn't love me enough."

2. "I'm unloved."

3. "I'm unwanted."

4. "I'm rejected."

5. "I'm on my own."

6. "I'm abandoned."

7. "Someone important left me."

8. "There's nobody there for me."

9. "I'm alone, lonely and/or isolated."

10. "There is something wrong with me."

11. "I'm bad."

12. "I'm not good enough."

13. "I've let others down."

14. "I'm let down by others."

15. "It should not have happened that way."

16. "I've lost someone/something I love."

17. "I feel bad for others."

18. "I'm not able to do what I want."

19. "I'm unprotected, unsafe, weak or vulnerable."

20. "I can't stop bad things happening."

Other Common Toxic Beliefs Include:

- "There's something wrong."
- "I'm weak."
- "I'm confused."
- "It's my fault."
- "I'm separate from the source of love."

Real-life Root-Cause Reasons justifying the most common toxic beliefs:

IMPORTANT: It is *not* recommended that you read through all of the following Root-Cause Reasons: they do not make for light reading! Just read the examples listed below of the toxic belief(s) that feel most true to you.

1   Real-life Root-Cause Reasons justifying the belief
     My parents did not love me enough
     include:
- "Sad not loved by Mum and Dad".
- "Hurt that Dad loves Mum more than me."
- "Sad Mum and Dad didn't care enough."
- "Sad, scared and vulnerable my parents didn't care about me."
- "Sad and vulnerable Dad didn't love me."
- "Hurt, sad and rejected Mum and Dad loved my brother more."
- "Sad, hurt and abandoned not cared about."
- "Sad Dad doesn't love me."
- "Sad Mum and Dad couldn't be bothered helping me."
- "Hurt, sad and scared Mum didn't want me."
- "Sad, scared and vulnerable Dad didn't fight for me."
- "Sad, alone and left out, parents didn't love me as much."

- ☐ "Hurt, sad and vulnerable Mum didn't love me."
- ☐ "Sad my parents preferred my brother."
- ☐ "Sad I don't feel loved and supported by Mum and Dad."
- ☐ "Hurt that my mum and dad resent me."
- ☐ "Angry and sad Mum and Dad didn't give a shit about me."
- ☐ "Sad Dad doesn't love me for who I am."
- ☐ "Hurt Mum didn't tell me she loved me."

2   Real-life Root-Cause Reasons justifying the belief
     I'm unloved
      include:
- ☐ "Left out and lonely not loved as much."
- ☐ "Hurt and angry not cared about."
- ☐ "Sad and alone not loved."
- ☐ "Sad I don't matter."
- ☐ "Alone and lonely because I'm not lovable."
- ☐ "Scared of not being loved."
- ☐ "Sad I don't know why I'm not liked."
- ☐ "Sad and scared not liked".
- ☐ "Sad, scared and vulnerable not loved by Mum."
- ☐ "I need to work hard in order to be loved."
- ☐ "Sad and useless not lovable as I am."
- ☐ "Hurt, sad and scared not lovable."

3   Real-life Root-Cause Reasons justifying the belief
     I'm unwanted
      include:
- ☐ "Sad treated so unfairly all the time because I'm not wanted."
- ☐ "Hurt and worthless not loved and accepted for who I am."
- ☐ "Hurt Mum and Dad didn't accept me."

- ☐ "Sad that I'm not wanted."
- ☐ "Scared that I'm not needed."
- ☐ "Empty because I don't matter."
- ☐ "Sad, vulnerable and scared that nobody wants me."
- ☐ "Lonely and isolated never good enough to have a best friend."
- ☐ "Hurt that I'm not noticed."
- ☐ "Feel worthless and not wanted."
- ☐ "Sad and angry that I don't matter."
- ☐ "Sad and worthless when people are happy without me."
- ☐ "Scared and alone because I'm not wanted."
- ☐ "Sad unwanted because I was a girl."
- ☐ "Hurt there's something wrong with me and I'm not wanted."
- ☐ "Sad Dad didn't want me."
- ☐ "Sad parents didn't want me."
- ☐ "Hurt, sad and vulnerable Mum and Dad sent me away."

4   Real-life Root-Cause Reasons justifying the belief
     I'm rejected
     include:
- ☐ "Hurt and rejected by people."
- ☐ "Hurt, rejected and worthless Mum doesn't love me."
- ☐ "Scared of being hurt and rejected by someone I love."
- ☐ "Sad, angry and worthless I was rejected and replaced."
- ☐ "Hurt and rejected because I was a girl."
- ☐ "Sad and rejected when misunderstood."
- ☐ "Sad my brother rejected me."
- ☐ "Sad rejected by Mum."
- ☐ "Sad, hurt, unwanted and rejected when people leave me."
- ☐ "Hurt rejected by my dad."

5   Real-life Root-Cause Reasons justifying the belief
      I'm on my own
      include:

☐ "Left out and alone."
☐ "Sad, scared and vulnerable on my own."
☐ "Scared when I'm on my own."
☐ "Lost, alone and lonely on my own."
☐ "Sad they are going to leave me on my own."
☐ "Scared and alone left on my own."
☐ "Isolated and vulnerable I'm on my own."
☐ "Helpless completely on my own."
☐ "Sad about being left out."
☐ "Sad, sick and lonely when I'm left to survive on my own."
☐ "Let down, lost and lonely left to get by on my own."
☐ "Sad, lonely, left alone and having to do things on my own."

6   Real-life Root-Cause Reasons justifying the belief
      I'm abandoned
      include:

☐ "Scared of being abandoned."
☐ "Sad everyone I love abandons me."
☐ "Sad and scared abandoned by my mum."
☐ "Hurt and angry that I was abandoned."
☐ "Abandoned in my moment of need."
☐ "Completely lost and abandoned not cared about."
☐ "Sad, lonely and helpless when abandoned and left behind."
☐ "Alone and abandoned not cared about."
☐ "Sad, shocked and confused abandoned by Mum."
☐ "Hurt, sad and scared not safe abandoned by Mum."
☐ "Terrified abandoned by Mum."

7   Real-life Root-Cause Reasons justifying the belief
Someone important left me
include:

- ☐ "Hurt, scared and alone when Mum left."
- ☐ "Sad Dad left me behind."
- ☐ "Sad, scared, alone and vulnerable when Dad left me."
- ☐ "Hurt and angry Mum and Dad left us."
- ☐ "Scared and hopeless when people I love leave."
- ☐ "Sad I miss the people I love."
- ☐ "Sad, scared and vulnerable parents left me on my own."
- ☐ "Sad, hurt and unwanted when people leave me."

8   Real-life Root-Cause Reasons justifying the belief
There's nobody there for me
include:

- ☐ "Sad nobody there for me."
- ☐ "Sad Dad wasn't there for me."
- ☐ "Sad, weak and rejected nobody there for me."
- ☐ "Sad and alone without my soulmate there for me."
- ☐ "Lost and alone nobody there for me."
- ☐ "Sad and lonely nobody there for me."
- ☐ "Sad, scared and vulnerable not looked after."
- ☐ "Sad, scared and vulnerable nobody there for me."
- ☐ "Sad, scared and alone nobody there for me."
- ☐ "Sad nobody there to help me."
- ☐ "Sad, lonely and isolated Mum and Dad not there for me."

9   Real-life Root-Cause Reasons justifying the belief
I'm alone, lonely and/or isolated
include:

- ☐ "Sad I'm so isolated."
- ☐ "Sad nobody to play with."
- ☐ "Lonely and isolated with no support."

☐ "Sad that I'm alone in the universe."
☐ "Sad and lonely my sister didn't want to be seen with me."
☐ "Sick, scared and vulnerable when left out and not liked."
☐ "Sad and lonely not seen or understood."
☐ "Sad and isolated when unfairly ganged up on."
☐ "Sad and helpless when people turn and walk away."
☐ "Left out and alone nobody to turn to."
☐ "Sad, lost and lonely nobody there for me."
☐ "Sad I had nobody."
☐ "Sad and lonely because I'm alone and not liked."
☐ "Lonely and isolated coz Mum and Dad split up."
☐ "Sad, lost and alone Dad's gone."
☐ "Sad and vulnerable Dad's gone."
☐ "Lonely and isolated because I should be something else".
☐ "Sad Dad not there to comfort me."
☐ "Sad and scared people think I'm disgusting and exclude me."
☐ "Sad and angry when separated from Mum."
☐ "Scared of being alone and lonely."
☐ "Sad, scared and isolated because I'm fat."

10   Real-life Root-Cause Reasons justifying the belief
     There's something wrong with me
     include:

☐ "Guilty because I should have been a boy."
☐ "Hurt, sad and angry always told something wrong with me."
☐ "Sad, scared and guilty there's something wrong with me."
☐ "Sad and frustrated always something wrong with me."
☐ "Scared of being exposed as a fraud."
☐ "Sad there's something wrong with me."
☐ "Hurt, angry and guilty made to feel dirty."
☐ "Shame from being violated and dirty."

- ☐ "Sad, scared and vulnerable when I do something wrong."
- ☐ "Upset that I felt stupid."
- ☐ "Angry made to look stupid."
- ☐ "Sad, alone and not lovable because I'm different."
- ☐ "Sad and lonely I'm different."

11 Real-life Root-Cause Reasons justifying the belief
    I'm bad
    include:

- ☐ "Sad I'm bad."
- ☐ "Sad not normal."
- ☐ "Sad I'm ugly."
- ☐ "Sad and guilty I'm naughty."
- ☐ "Sad I don't deserve to be alive."
- ☐ "Sad and ashamed because I'm stupid."
- ☐ "Hurt, sad and guilty that I'm bad."
- ☐ "Hurt, isolated and alone there's something wrong with me."
- ☐ "I'm worthless compared to others."
- ☐ "Sad I'm a bad person."
- ☐ "Hurt, sad and worthless I'm not doing it right."

12 Real-life Root-Cause Reasons justifying the belief
    I'm not good enough
    include:

- ☐ "Sad never good enough for Dad."
- ☐ "Hurt about not being good enough."
- ☐ "Deflated that my best is never good enough."
- ☐ "I'm not good enough to meet my soulmate."
- ☐ "Sad not good enough for other people to want to be with me."
- ☐ "Sad never good enough for the people I love."
- ☐ "I'm shit and worthless compared to others."
- ☐ "Sad I'm always second best."

- ☐ "Sad and isolated because I'm not important."
- ☐ "Hurt always wrong and never good enough for Mum."
- ☐ "Sad and rejected because I'm not good enough."

13 Real-life Root-Cause Reasons justifying the belief
I've let others down
include:
- ☐ "Sad let Dad down."
- ☐ "Sad and guilty that Dad has never been proud of me."
- ☐ "Sad let my mum down."
- ☐ "Sad and guilty I disappointed my dad."
- ☐ "Panic about letting Dad down."
- ☐ "Sad and guilty that I've failed and let my parents down."
- ☐ "Sad that I've let my parents down."
- ☐ "Feel really bad that I've hurt my mum."
- ☐ "Sad and guilty not there for my mum."
- ☐ "Sad I couldn't help Mum."
- ☐ "Sad and guilty I couldn't save my parents."
- ☐ "Sad that I've not been there for my mum."
- ☐ "Scared to let people down."

14 Real-life Root-Cause Reasons justifying the belief
I'm let down by others
include:
- ☐ "Sad let down by the people I love."
- ☐ "Scared of being hurt by people close to me."
- ☐ "Lost, alone and let down by partner."
- ☐ "Hurt about being let down."
- ☐ "Sad and lonely nobody understood me."
- ☐ "Hurt Mum always put herself first."
- ☐ "Hurt, angry and disgusted at Dad."
- ☐ "Let down that Dad was so selfish."
- ☐ "Scared Dad wasn't in control."
- ☐ "Sad Dad never supported me."

- ☐ "Hurt and sad that Dad was mean to me."
- ☐ "Angry Dad bullied the confidence out of me."
- ☐ "Hate Dad dominating me."
- ☐ "Hurt let down by Dad."
- ☐ "Pissed off because I hate Dad's wife."
- ☐ "Angry I never got support."
- ☐ "Sad and scared Dad left me alone with Mum."
- ☐ "Hurt, stupid and worthless when brother put me down."
- ☐ "Sad, scared and alone when betrayed by partner."
- ☐ "Angry people do things I don't want them to do."

> REMEMBER: You are a good person. You always do your best. Your intentions are positive. And nothing can ever impact your lovability.

15   Real-life Root-Cause Reasons justifying the belief
It should not have happened that way
include:

- ☐ "Sad I didn't get to know my mum."
- ☐ "Sad I've wasted my life."
- ☐ "Sad my kids don't have grandparents."
- ☐ "Sad I got rid of my first baby."
- ☐ "Shame and guilt that I let X abuse me for so long."
- ☐ "Sad, lost and alone falling apart after abortion."
- ☐ "Sad Dad died before I got to know him."
- ☐ "Sad that I shouldn't have been born."
- ☐ "Sad I wasn't close to my parents."
- ☐ "Sad missed out on attention from my mum."
- ☐ "Sad he/she couldn't come to me for help."
- ☐ "Angry because I was forced to do things I didn't want to do."
- ☐ "Sad and guilty I was too busy and missed time with my child."

16 Real-life Root-Cause Reasons justifying the belief
    I've lost someone/something I love
    include:
- [ ] "Sad I lost my dad."
- [ ] "Sad and overwhelmed I've lost the people I love."
- [ ] "Sad, scared and alone when I lose the people I love."
- [ ] "Hurt, sad and scared that people I love leave me."
- [ ] "Sad I lost my brother."
- [ ] "Empty when I lose the people I love."
- [ ] "Sad, left out and lonely when people I love are taken away."
- [ ] "Sad and scared of losing people I love."
- [ ] "Sad to lose people I love."
- [ ] "Sad and scared everything was breaking down."
- [ ] "Sad and scared about losing Dad's love."
- [ ] "Hurt because the people I love don't love me enough to stay."
- [ ] "Sad I lost my child and missed out on having a family."

17 Real-life Root-Cause Reasons justifying the belief
    I feel bad for others
    include:
- [ ] "Sad my dad was so weak and vulnerable.'
- [ ] "Sad and scared Dad was so pathetic."
- [ ] "Sad my dad is sad."
- [ ] "Sad and scared to see Dad hurt and vulnerable."
- [ ] "Tired of carrying my dad's heaviness."
- [ ] "Sad and scared to see Mum so weak."
- [ ] "Sad and guilty to see my mum hurting."
- [ ] "Sad and alone Mum gets upset and can't help me."
- [ ] "Sad and weak not able to help my mum."
- [ ] "Sad and scared to see Dad so ill and weak."
- [ ] "Scared of Mum being upset."

- ☐ "Angry Mum's parents hurt my mum."
- ☐ "Sad and helpless to see my dad suffering."
- ☐ "Sad and scared Mum so vulnerable."

18   Real-life Root-Cause Reasons justifying the belief
I'm not able to do what I want
include:

- ☐ "Stuck and helpless not free to do what I want."
- ☐ "Hate being told what to do."
- ☐ "Angry not able to do what I want."
- ☐ "Sad and stuck not free to be me."
- ☐ "Pissed off at petty rules."
- ☐ "Sad they don't care about what I want."
- ☐ "Hurt not allowed to do what I want to do."
- ☐ "Helpless I can't do anything to fix it."
- ☐ "Scared and powerless not able to stop bad things happening."
- ☐ "Sad and angry not able to complete my life purpose."
- ☐ "I'm frustrated that I'm not able to do what I want."

> REMEMBER: If you want to see something inspirational, then look in a mirror! You have already accomplished so much with your life. You are more confident than you think. You can do it!

19   Real-life Root-Cause Reasons justifying the belief
I'm unprotected, unsafe, weak or vulnerable
include:

- ☐ "Sad and vulnerable Mum didn't protect me."
- ☐ "Lonely and vulnerable Dad not there."
- ☐ "Let down and vulnerable brother didn't protect me."
- ☐ "Scared, vulnerable and unprotected."
- ☐ "Sad I was violated."

- ☐ "Scared that people will see that I'm vulnerable."
- ☐ "Scared and helpless I couldn't stop them hurting me."
- ☐ "Scared of being exposed."
- ☐ "Scared and alone struggling for life."
- ☐ "Scared and vulnerable Dad's so unpredictable."
- ☐ "Hurt, scared and helpless couldn't tell him to stop."
- ☐ "Scared and vulnerable when out of control."
- ☐ "Scared and weak when people see I'm weak."
- ☐ "Scared left alone with nobody to protect me."
- ☐ "Hurt, unprotected and violated."
- ☐ "Sad and scared helpless and vulnerable."
- ☐ "Hurt and isolated not safe."
- ☐ "Sad I couldn't stop my dad from hurting me."
- ☐ "Scared of being weak."
- ☐ "Sad and alone nobody there to stick up for me."
- ☐ "Scared to be weak and crumble."
- ☐ "Scared of being hurt when exposed and open."
- ☐ "Vulnerable when I'm outside my home."
- ☐ "Scared of people seeing me."
- ☐ "Scared and vulnerable of Dad hurting me."
- ☐ "Scared my life is so vulnerable."
- ☐ "Tired of feeling suffocated and powerless."
- ☐ "Vulnerable when people invade my space."
- ☐ "Sad and frightened not protected by Dad."
- ☐ "Scared, alone and vulnerable nobody there to protect me."

20 Real-life Root-Cause Reasons justifying the belief
    I can't stop bad things happening
    include:

- ☐ "Scared of being hurt."
- ☐ "Sad and scared of getting things wrong."
- ☐ "Scared to be homeless."
- ☐ "Scared I'm going to die."

- ☐ "Sad and scared to lose my safety net."
- ☐ "Scared of being stuck."
- ☐ "Scared something bad is going to happen."
- ☐ "Scared people I love could get hurt."
- ☐ "Sad and scared of being abused."
- ☐ "Scared of hurting my kids in the same way I was hurt."
- ☐ "Scared to get it wrong and hurt the people I love."
- ☐ "Scared of Mum and Dad splitting up."
- ☐ "Petrified of getting ill like my mother."
- ☐ "Scared of losing what I've got."
- ☐ "Scared of losing my mum and dad."
- ☐ "Scared that I will end up like Mum."
- ☐ "Scared I can't cope."
- ☐ "Scared of screwing up."
- ☐ "Sad and scared that I'm going to get into trouble."

REMEMBER: Holding grudges hurts the hands that hold them. You do not have to agree with the actions of others to heal your relationship with the past. Compassion sets you free!

Next Steps

· · · · · ·

Inspired to learn and experience more? Here's what to do:

Join My Members-Only Online Club

My Calm Clan has *made Mind Detox mobile* as it consists of online meditations, workshops, gatherings and resources. Inside you can "heal for real" by taking online courses in Mind Detox, Mind Calm, Body Calm and Calm Cure. As a member you get unlimited access to hundreds of hours of teaching videos, guided meditations and weekly live broadcasts with me, my team of Calmologists and guest experts. My Calm Clan is the easiest and cheapest way to learn Calmology and receive the support you need in meditation, Mind Detox and life.

For more info visit: **www.calmclan.com**

Train with My Academy

Would you like to gain the ability to share Calmology with others? My Academy offers home-study certification courses in Mind Detox, Mind Calm, Body Calm and Calm Cure. Millions of people need Mind Detox, crave more calm in their lives and are waiting to learn meditation and experience Mind Detox from you!

Train and qualify with my Academy to study at home and change the world! **www.calmacademy.com**

One-to-One Coaching

To work with me privately, one to one, please visit my website and book one of my coaching or mentoring packages.

Courses and Retreats

I run courses in meditation and Mind Detox along with retreats. During a long weekend in the UK or a longer retreat at my international venues, you will have the opportunity to learn from my team and me, which will deepen your understanding and experience significantly.

Ascension Courses

My original meditation technique is known as Ascension, as taught by the Ishayas of The Bright Path. I am an Ishaya Monk and qualified teacher of the Ascension techniques. I credit much of what I've learned about peace, freedom and conscious living to my Ascension practice and guidance from my Spiritual Teacher, M.K.I. I highly recommend you learn to "ascend" if you have a desire to know what it means to be truly alive and would value a path that can help you to wake up and be free.

For more info about my other books, coaching, retreats and courses, to access an online directory listing the common causes of physical and emotional conditions and access free resources on the topics covered within this book, visit my website: **www.sandynewbigging.com**

Acknowledgements

· · · · · ·

THANKS to all at Findhorn Press and Inner Traditions for publishing the second edition of this book. I would especially like to thank Sabine Weeke for her patience, support and continued belief in me and my work.

Very special thanks to Maharani. You have given me the time and support I needed when writing this book. You surprise me every day and I love you more every moment.

Special thanks to Becci Godfrey for your endless encouragement and clarifying conversations.

I would also like to thank my family – Mum, Dad, Max, Sam and Amber – and every single person who's attended one of my clinics, courses or retreats – including the members of my Calm Clan, the Academy students and the growing team of Calmologists.

Thank you to my Ishaya family for the fun conversations that stretch my consciousness.

Finally, infinite love and gratitude, as always, go to my Spiritual Teacher, MKI. You have taught me that peace is possible, irrespective of what life brings. It is a priceless and glorious gift.